CANDLESTICK TRADING

A Comprehensive Beginner's Guide to Learn the
Realms of Candlestick Trading from A to Z

KEVIN BAILEY

Contents

Introduction

In comparison to a line chart, bar chart, or point and figure chart, candlesticks are the most preferred chart among traders. It has gained appeal among traders since it visually provides a wide range of trading information in one go. Candlestick charts are also easy to understand and read. It is made up of two parts: the body (rectangle component of the candle) and the shadow (wicks) (lines above or below the body). Each candlestick also has a price for the open, high, low, and close. The timeframe of the candlestick chart is set by the trader based on his trading horizon.

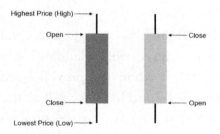

Many technical analysis patterns and trends are named for the shapes they resemble when viewed in chart form. Many people believe that this is the simplest form of technical analysis chart to interpret for beginners. New investors must understand the meaning of each piece of chart data. The primary section of the candlestick's shape is known as the body or actual body, and it can be solid or hollow in either case. Long, narrow lines are always tied to bodies at the top and bottom, and these are known as shadows, wicks, or tails. Typically, the shadow represents the stock's peak and low price ranges.

If you wanted to make a candlestick chart without using a computer tracking program, you'd need a data set containing the daily open, low, high, and close values for each period of time you wanted to study, whether it was a single day, a week, or a year. Once you have this information, you can start recording it on the chart in the form of candlestick shapes so that you may conduct a more thorough analysis. If a stock finished at a price that was greater than its opening price, you would draw a candlestick with a hollow body. The opening price would be represented by the bottom edge of the body, while the closing price would be represented by the top edge of the body. If you knew the stock had closed at a lower price than it had opened, you'd draw a filled candlestick with the top of the body representing the opening price and the bottom of the body representing the closing price.

To perform technical analysis on a stock, technical analysts need the least amount of data feasible. Candlestick charting is easy to understand and analyze while also providing information on the stock's open, close highs and lows, as well as the level of activity. The candles used in the charts, on the other hand, resemble a candle with a wick at each end. The wicks are usually referred to as shadows, while the full body of the candle is referred to as the true body. Each day might be represented by a candle on the chart. The open and close prices are shown at the top and bottom of the candle's body, while the highs and lows of the stock are shown in the shadows.

The candles can be black or white, or even red and green in some charts. When a candle is black or red, it means the stock closed lower than it opened. If it's white or green, that means the stock closed higher than where it started. The length of the candle body indicates how much trading activity the stock experienced throughout the day. The many permutations that the candles can display provide significant information to the investor. This is why candlestick charts are the most widely used technical analysis tool. This book will teach you all you need to know about candlestick trading and how to trade like an expert.

What Is Candlestick Trading?

Before I go into detail about candlestick trading, I think it's only fair to discuss candlestick charts and how they came to be

When employed appropriately, the combined power of western technical and candlestick analysis is a force to be reckoned with when evaluating a possible trade. Although candlestick trading tactics have only lately become popular in the western trading industry (since the 1980s), the Japanese have been using them to trade rice contracts for hundreds of years. Candlestick patterns indicate who is in the power of the current market in an instant and visually, i.e., "bulls or bears."

Candlestick charting is a type of charting that is similar to a bar chart in that it is used to examine supply and demand. The candlestick chart displays the same information as the bar chart, but it concentrates on the relationship between opening and closing prices. The candlestick approach is beneficial to investors because it allows them to perceive prices from a different perspective, and many investors find it easier to read.

Candlestick patterns should never be traded on their own, no matter how appealing the situation appears to be. Candlestick patterns are quite good at predicting price reversals in advance, but they don't tell you how big the reversal will be. Western technical indicators usually play a significant role in the final decision, guiding the trader in deciding whether or not to follow the reversal shown by the candlestick pattern.

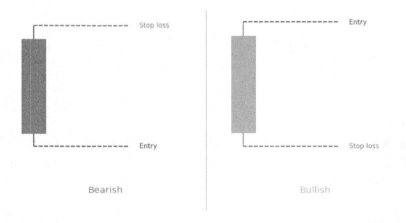

Traders use technical analysis to seek for different trading signals to enter a trade when the price is overbought or oversold. Traders use candle patterns to identify early price reversals. However, there is a powerful candlestick pattern that is rarely discussed, and many traders fail to see it when signal trading or doing trade analysis. The "inner candle reversal pattern" is what it's called.

A candle that forms inside the previous candle is known as an inside candle. The highs and lows of an inside candle must never surpass those of the previous candle; nevertheless, this powerful reversal pattern is only acceptable if it occurs quickly after an overbought or oversold position has arisen; otherwise, inside candlestick trading is not recommended.

Trading with candlesticks gives distinct visual indicators that make reading price action much easier. Speculators can better understand market mood by selling and buying with Japanese Candle Charts. Candlesticks emphasize a good way to the relationship between close price and open price, providing more depth of information than typical bar charts, which focus on the high and low. Candlestick traders can more quickly recognize various types of price action that tend to foretell trend reversals or continuations, which is one of the most difficult aspects of trading. When combined with other technical analysis tools, Candlestick pattern analysis can be a very useful tool for determining entry and exit locations. The body of a candlestick represents the difference between the open and closing price. Its hue (typically red for down and blue for up) indicates whether the market closed up or down for the day (or week, or year). The wicks (or shadows) identify the currency's extremely low and high prices on a given day.

The true body can be the essence of price movement, according to candlestick traders. When looking at data on a bar chart, you can use spikes to highlight highs and lows; however, these highs and lows are generally just market noise and have no bearing on excellent analysis. The power of candles is their capacity to visually check out this static and focus on what the market might force price, which is a smart thing to do during a trading stage just outside the trading pit. Technical analysis is the only approach to determine market sentiment. A candlestick by itself does not provide a lot of information for determining market sentiment. Professional traders, on the other hand, search for certain candlestick patterns to predict future price moves. Most of these candlesticks have unusual names based on their Japanese titles, such as Morning Star, Dark Cloud Cover, or Engulfing Pattern. Market emotion is often reflected in the names. Identifying changes in the direction of price activity is one of the most important tasks of technical analysis. One of the most useful elements of candlestick findings in terms of giving insight into what the market is thinking is their ability to suggest shifts in market sentiment. Reversal Patterns are the name given to these candle shapes.

Many reversal patterns, such as Head & Shoulders and Double Tops, may be found in western technical analysis. Those patterns are regular patterns noticed in price action that foreshadow a crisis, and they don't always provide much insight into what the market is thinking. In western analysis, reversal patterns might take a long time to establish. On the other hand, Candlestick interpretations place a greater emphasis on market psychology than the others. And, because the vast majority of Candlestick patterns endure only one to three time periods, traders can get a more accurate view of market mood in real-time. It's important to remember that a reversal pattern in candlesticks does not always indicate a complete trend reversal but rather a change or pause in the path. That might imply anything from a halt in development to sideways trade following an established trend or a complete reversal adjacent to a reversal candle template.

Continuation patterns indicate that the market will continue on its current path. Frequently, the candlesticks themselves are pointing in the opposite direction of the prevailing trend. Traders can use continuation patterns to tell the difference between a price action that is fully reversing and one that is only applying an intermission. The majority of traders will tell you that there is a time to trade and a time to rest. Consolidation, or a time to rest and watch, is implied by the emergence of continuation candlestick patterns. Candlesticks are a useful tool for gaining market knowledge. However, most candlestick analysts advise against using them as your sole technical analysis tool. Outside of what candle formations can tell you, technical analysis events frequently render these patterns meaningless.

History of Candlestick Trading

The candlestick method of technical analysis has its origins in
Japan and is now widely utilized
and popular all over the world. On
paper and in ancient Japanese
manuscripts, there are several
candlestick patterns that shed light
on the idea and fundamentals of it.

The Japanese rice trade in the seventeenth century was conducted using this method of technical investigation. Charles Dow is said to have utilized this to develop a modern version of candlestick technical analysis in the United States in 1900. But it is Homma, a rice dealer from Sakata, who deserves all of the credit for this charting technique.

This method is very beneficial for obtaining accurate low, high, close, and open prices within a specified timeframe. The candle's shadow represents low and high price points, while its body represents the opening and closing prices. The pricing is shaded in one direction or the other. When a candle is shaded down-wards, it means the stock's closing price was lower than its opening price.

Similarly, a candle that is shaded upwards demonstrates the inverse. The initial price was lower than the final price, as shown. Candlestick technical analysis comes in a variety of forms, each of which is used by different people for different reasons. As if there were a variety of patterns and colors used for shading.

. . .

Japan's Trading Genius

Homma's candlestick chart approach allowed him to profit from dozens of transactions in succession (some sources say over 100 in a row). He is said to have made almost $100 billion in today's money as a result of his actions. This would make Homma the world's most successful merchant and trader.

Homma went above and beyond just trading with the audience. He discovered a means to accurately observe the masses' behavior and exploit it to his benefit. He kept track of the opening and closing prices, as well as the day's high and low, and plotted them on a chart. This visual representation consisted of a series of columns that resembled candlesticks, hence the name.

Homma equated the conflict between buyers and sellers to warfare fought on old Japanese battlefields in his descriptions. Many of his pattern names are inspired by military notions. In English-speaking countries, these are known as the Three Soldiers and the Belt Hold Line, respectively. Other patterns, such as the Doji and the Harami, are still labelled in Japanese.

Homma's innovations made candlestick charting resemble the charts we use today in many ways. However, advancements in technology have made it an even more precise instrument for current traders.

Candlestick Charting in the Modern World

Despite its enormous popularity in Japan, candlestick charts were not frequently used in the West until roughly twenty-five years ago. They are now utilized all around the world as price prediction tools (and often merely for their graphic, eye-pleasing appeal).

Steve Nison wrote an essay about Japanese candlestick pattern analysis in Futures magazine in 1989. This publicity aided in the system's adoption in the United States. Nison is still regarded as one of the main authorities on the application of these charts to market analysis. **Here are some of his works that I recommend reading:**

- Strategies for Profiting with Japanese Candlestick Charts

- New Japanese Charting Techniques Revealed: Beyond Candlesticks

Candlestick pattern charts have become an important feature of western market analysis in recent years, thanks to these books and Nison's continuous trading success. With the rise of web-based trading, this absorption process has intensified since 2000.

Candlestick Chart in the 21st Century

 Since the internet's inception, the utilization of candlestick patterns has evolved significantly. Wide-spread information access and the merging of candlestick charts with various forms of analysis drive this dynamic innovation process. The addition of colors, which was made very recently, is one of the most intriguing additions. These color indicators might assist you in identifying crucial spots or days on the chart that may signal a future trend change. On the other hand, traditional Japanese candlestick patterns solely utilize black and white to depict trading ranges.

The white candles (good days) in several charts have now been replaced by hollow candles that are colorless. For gloomy days, red is commonly chosen, and these candles are usually solidly loaded. You might also notice a red candle that is hollow (red as just an outline). This denotes a complicated situation, **such as a day in which all of the following factors were present:**

- The opening was lower than the close of the previous day.
- Despite this, the market was positive.

- It didn't finish the day trading higher than the previous day's close.

A day of decision with a black-filled candle would be one in which there was a "gap" in trade in the other direction. For example, the current close was higher than the prior close, while the day opened higher than the previous close. The concept of gap trading is introduced into candlestick charts with this update. The notion is that all trading gaps tend to close over time.

Types of Candlestick Patterns

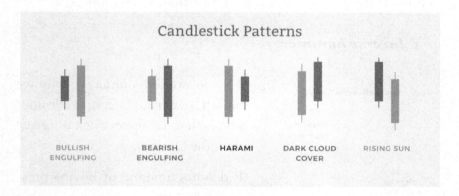

It's crucial to note that, while candlestick patterns are wonderful for quickly identifying trends, they should be used in conjunction with other forms of technical analysis to corroborate the overall trend.

Six Bullish Candlestick Patterns

After a market decline, bullish patterns may appear, signaling a price reversal. They are a signal for traders to open a long position in order to profit from any rising trend.

- ### *Hammer*

At the bottom of a downward trend, the hammer candlestick pattern is formed by a short body with a long lower wick.

A hammer indicates that the price eventually rose despite selling forces during the day due to signifi-

cant purchasing pressure. The body color varies, but green hammers signal a stronger bull market than red hammers.

- ### *Inverse hammer*

The inverted hammer is another bullish pattern. The only distinction is that the upper wick is longer than the lower wick.

It denotes a period of buying pressure followed by a period of selling pressure that was insufficient to force the market price down. The inverse hammer indicates that buyers will take control of the market in the near future.

- ### *Bullish engulfing.*

Two candlesticks constitute the bullish engulfing pattern. A smaller red candle gets fully consumed by a larger green candle in the first candle.

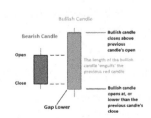

Despite the fact that the second day begins lower than the first, the bullish market drives the price upward, resulting in a clear gain for buyers.

- *Piercing line.*

Piercing Line Pattern
- Two candle Pattern
- Trend Reversal Pattern
- Effective if found during down trend
- 1st Candle: Red (Bearish)
- 2nd Candle: Green (Bullish)
- Both candles should be big
- Green candle opens below Red candle.
- Green candle closes slightly below the top of Red candle.

The piercing line is a two-stick pattern as well, consisting of a long red candle followed by a long green candle.

Between the closing price of the first candlestick and the opening price of the green candlestick, there is frequently a large difference. The price is pushed up to or above the previous day's mid-price, indicating strong purchasing pressure.

- *Morning star.*

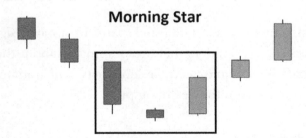

Morning Star

In a dark market decline, the morning star candlestick pattern is seen as a symbol of hope. It's a three-stick pattern with one short-bodied candle sandwiched between two long red and green candles. Because the market gaps are both on open and close, the 'star' will typically have no overlap with the lengthier bodies.

It indicates that the selling pressure from the first day has subsided and that a bull market is approaching.

- ***Three white soldiers,***

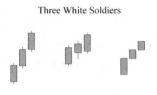

Three White Soldiers

The pattern of the three white troops lasts three days. It consists of a series of tall green (or white) candles with short wicks that open and close higher each day than the day before.

After a decline, a very strong bullish signal appears, indicating a sustained increase of buying pressure.

Six Bearish Candlestick Patterns

After an ascent, bearish candlestick patterns appear, signaling a point of resistance. Traders that are pessimistic about the market price would often liquidate their long bets and initiate a short position to profit from the declining price.

- ***Hanging man.***

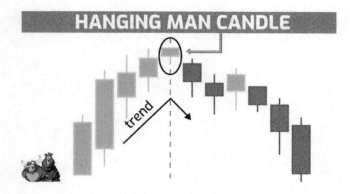

The bearish analogue of a hammer is the hanging man; it has the same shape as a hammer but appears at the end of an uptrend.

It suggests that there was a substantial sell-off earlier in the day but that buyers were able to bring the price back up. The sharp drop is frequently interpreted as a sign that the bulls are losing control of the market.

- ***Shooting star.***

The shooting star has a smaller lower body and a longer upper wick than the inverted hammer, but it is generated in an uptrend.

Typically, the market will begin slightly higher, climb to an intra-day high, and then close at a price just above the open — like a falling star.

- ***Bearish engulfing.***

At the end of an upswing, a bearish engulfing pattern appears. The first candle has a small green body, which is devoured by a lengthy red candle that follows.

It denotes a price peak or slowdown and is a warning indicator of an imminent market decline. The trend is more likely to be substantial the lower the second candle descends.

- *Evening star.*

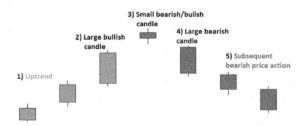

The evening star is a three-candlestick pattern that is the bearish morning star's counterpart. A short candle is placed between a tall green candle and a large red candlestick in this arrangement.

It denotes the conclusion of an uptrend and is especially powerful when the third candlestick wipes out the gains of the first.

- ***Three black crows.***

Three consecutive long red candles with short or non-existent wicks make up the three black crows candlestick motif. Each session begins at a similar price as the previous one, but selling pressures drive the price lower with each closing.

Traders view this pattern as the commencement of a bearish slump, as sellers have outpaced purchases for three trading days in a row.

- ***Dark cloud cover.***

A bearish reversal is indicated by the dark cloud cover candlestick pattern, which is a dark cloud over the previous day's optimism. It consists of two candlesticks: a red candlestick that opens above the previous green body and closes below its midpoint. A green candlestick opens above the previous green body and closes below its halfway.

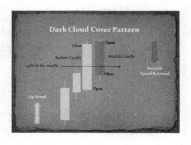

It indicates that the bears have gained control of the session and are driving the market lower. If the candles' wicks are short, it indicates that the downturn was very strong.

Four Continuation Candlestick Patterns

A continuation pattern occurs when a candlestick pattern does not suggest a shift in market direction. When there is market hesitation or neutral price movement, these might help traders detect a time of market rest.

- ### *Doji*

When a market's open and close are almost equal, the candlestick resembles a cross or plus sign; traders should look for a short to the non-existent body with various length wicks.

The pattern of this Doji depicts a fight between buyers and sellers, with no net gain for either side. Although a Doji is a neutral indicator, it can be found in reversal patterns like the bullish morning star and bearish evening star.

- ### *Spinning Top.*

A short body is located between wicks of equal length in the spinning top candlestick style. The pattern implies market hesitation, resulting in no major price change: the bulls drove the price higher, while the bears drove it back down. Following a big rally or slump, spinning tops are sometimes viewed as a period of consolidation or rest.

The spinning top is a pretty benign signal on its own, but it can be regarded as a portent of things to come because it indicates that market pressure is losing control.

- **Falling three methods.**

The continuation of a present trend, whether bearish or bullish, is predicted using three-method formation patterns.

The 'falling three techniques,' a bearish pattern, is known. It's made up of a long red body, three little green bodies, and another red body – the green candles are all contained inside the bearish body's range. It demonstrates to traders that the bulls lack the necessary strength to reverse the trend.

- **Raised three methods.**

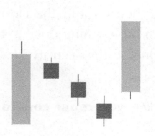

The bullish pattern, also known as the "rising three methods" candlestick pattern, is the polar opposite. It's made up of three short reds wedged between two long greens. Traders can see from the pattern that, despite some selling pressure, buyers are still in charge of the market.

The Importance of Candlestick Patterns

Have you ever wondered how stock market analysts decide whether or not to sell or trade stocks? It's quite difficult for them to predict which stocks will sell the most and which will have a surplus. Understanding the market flow is necessary for forecasting future sales and increasing profits, but how will they do so if they only see numbers? This is why candlestick patterns are important because they show how the market is moving and are thus a vital tool for brokers to utilize in the stock market battlefield.

Homma Munehisa, a Japanese trader, invented candlestick charts in the 18th century. The charts provided the famed trader and others with a visual representation of open, high, low, and closing market prices over time. This charting technique has gained a lot of popularity due to how simple it is to read and interpret graphs. In addition, the patterns that resulted gave a solid forecast of future demand.

The body of a candlestick is made up of a body and an upper and lower shadow or wick. During the time span depicted, the wick represents the greatest and lowest traded values of security. The starting and closing trades are depicted in the body. The body is unfilled or white if the security closed higher than it opened, with the opening price at the bottom and the closing price at the top. The body is black, with the opening price at the top and the closing price at the bottom of the security closed lower than it opened.

And, in order to predict the stock market, **you must consider its formation and analysis:**

- **Candlesticks Formations.** A combination of

different candlesticks represents a day in a weekly or monthly interval. This graph depicts the stock market's demand movement. The shape also represents the stock market's flow, indicating when there is a high demand or when there is a high surplus. This structure substantially aids analysts and dealers in making informed decisions about which equities to sell or keep.

- **Candlesticks Analysis.** It's the resultant conclusion or hypothesis about how the stock market has performed. When there is a high demand, how high the demand was, and the interval or length of time there is a high demand or even a high excess is all included in this report. This is a statement on the meaning of the candlestick pattern. As a result, candlestick analysis is a key skill that brokers employ to predict the market effectively.

Certainly, the stock market is not for everyone, and it is not a place where you can make catastrophic mistakes. Because the environment is so volatile, even a minor blunder can result in significant losses. It is critical to have a thorough understanding of candlestick patterns or formations, as well as the analysis that the latter will provide. Because if this market is not given enough weight, brokers and investors may be unable to profit from it.

Benefits of Candlestick

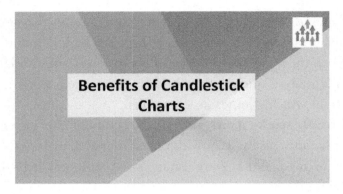

What advantages do candlestick charts have over traditional high-low bar charts? Nothing is displayed as far as the actual data is concerned. Candlestick charts, like bar charts, show the open, high, low, and close for security.

On the other hand, Candlesticks are considerably superior to typical bar charts in terms of visual identification of data and the capacity to see data correlations and investor emotion over time.

- ***Superior to traditional charts.***

On the other hand, Candlestick charts illustrate the movement in the market that day in considerably greater depth than traditional bar charts. Pattern analysis can be used to assess the possibility of future movement in equity by looking at its price action over time. Candlestick chart pattern analysis can play an important role in almost any investment strategy with little experience and familiarization.

- ***Psychological portrait.***

We all know that fear, greed, and hope all have an impact on prices. To comprehend these shifting psychological elements, some type of technical analysis is required. Candlesticks can be used to read changes in the market's value determination, often known as investor mood. Candlesticks depict buyer-seller interaction, which is frequently reflected in price movement. As a result, candlestick charts reveal information about the financial markets that regular bar charts do not.

- *Easy to understand.*

Candlesticks are a visual representation of a series of patterns that are extremely accurate in anticipating market trends. You may immediately begin to notice patterns form in the market by utilizing candlesticks in conjunction with some basic technical analysis — and, more crucially, you can start taking advantage of these patterns when you trade.

Candlesticks have the advantage of not taking months or years to master. The patterns can be memorized pretty rapidly with practice, and while this does require some effort, the profit potential of learning these techniques is priceless. Candlestick charts have been used to help traders comprehend market price action for over 250 years.

How Does a Candlestick Work?

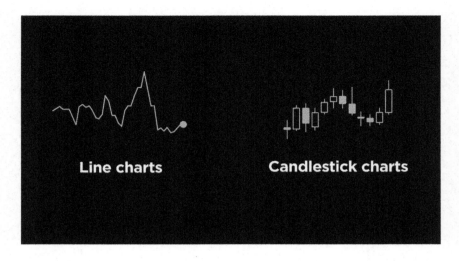

Candlesticks can reveal more than merely price change over time. To sense market emotion and make forecasts about where the market might go next, experienced traders search for patterns. **Here are a few examples of what they're looking for:**

A long wick on the bottom of a candle, for example, might indicate that traders are buying into an asset as prices fall, which could be a sign that the asset is on the rise.

A lengthy wick at the top of a candle, on the other hand, could indicate that traders are eager to profit, indicating a huge potential sell-off coming up soon.

Assume that the body takes up nearly the entire candle, with very short wicks (or none at all) on either side. That could imply a strong bullish (on a green candle) or bearish (on a red candle) mood (on a red candle).

Understanding what candlesticks represent in the context of a specific asset or market conditions is one component of technical analysis, a trading approach in which investors seek to detect trends and potential future opportunities by analyzing past price movements.

What are "one-candle signals?" and how do you read them?

Traders that trade in very short time frames may focus on just one candle at a time. As a beginner, familiarizing yourself with these "one-candle signals" can be beneficial. **Four frequent one-candle signals are listed below:**

A long upper shadow may signal a bearish trend, indicating that traders are eager to sell and profit. The stronger the indicator, the longer the upper shadow.

A long lower shadow could be a bullish indication, indicating that investors are looking to buy and pushing prices higher. The signal is more reliable if the shadow is longer and lower.

Because the open and close prices are the same, a Doji candle has no body. These are often seen as market indecision and are a probable indicator of a price reversal on the horizon. (What is the significance of the term "Doji?") Japanese rice traders first utilized candlestick charts in the 18th century. "Doji" means "mistake," perhaps because prices rarely open and close in the same location.)

The bottom wick of an umbrella is unusually lengthy. A hammer is another name for a red umbrella. When you see a hammer, it usually signifies that the asset is seeing a lot of buyer interest and that the price is about to rise. Green umbrellas, on the other hand, are known as "hanging men." They're frequently a hint that sellers are ready to sell, reversing the uptrend.

It's crucial to remember that one-candle indications might be useful, but a correct market reading necessitates comprehension of the bigger picture. It's not easy to discern trends and patterns in candlestick charts. Consult a professional advisor if you're unsure about which investment approach is best for you.

There are only three basic stages to identifying a **trend on a candlestick chart:**

- First, take a brief look at the chart. Is the stock rising, falling, or moving sideways?
- Second, we zoom in and examine the trend's intermediate-term peaks and troughs.
- Finally, we combine steps one and two to create an educated prediction as to where we are in the trend right now: are we approaching a low or a high?

Peaks and Valleys, Highs and Lows

So now we have a good idea of where the trend is going. To better grasp how the trend is playing out, we'll need to do some basic trend analysis.

When it comes to mountains, you're definitely familiar with the concept of peaks and valleys. Mountains feature very high peaks, which are frequently followed by valleys, which are considerably lower points. Few, if any, mountains ascend in a straight line. Even the strongest trends will have small pullbacks; the same is true for equities.

Peaks and valleys in stock trends, in my opinion, are the most significant component of trend research. It's high-level data that conveys the complete narrative. **The trend study can be summarized using the following maxim:**

- Higher highs and lower lows define an uptrend.
- Lower highs and lower lows define a downtrend.

To put it another way, a strong stock trend is defined by not only high peaks, but each peak and valley is higher than the one before it.

A significant upswing can be seen in the chart below. Sure, the stock still drops and forms a valley (or a trough, depending on how you look at it), but each subsequent peak and valley is higher than the last.

When a trend fails to make a higher high or lower low, it should be regarded as weakened at best and reversed at worst. These aren't the best trend situations to invest in.

2

Tips On How To Trade
Candlestick Pattern

C andlestick patterns are one of the most widely utilized technical analysis concepts. Simultaneously, there are several misunderstandings and half-truths circulating, resulting in uncertainty and poor trading decisions. Different perspectives on candlestick analysis are presented below; along with explanations of the most typical issues traders face while trading price action.

Different perspectives on candlestick analysis are presented below; along with explanations of the most typical issues traders face while trading price action.

- ***Evening star – Abandoned baby.***

On daily charts, the abandoned baby or evening star is most typically seen, but a slightly modified variation can also be found on lower timeframes.

Candle **sequence and formation:**

- **During a positive trend:** A enormous red candle

26

with a gap lower – a long green candle – a very little candle with a gap up.

- **During a bear market:** A enormous green candle with a gap up – a long red candle – a very small candle with a gap down.

The gap is not required, and the candle sequence is the most important aspect of this pattern. The small candle between the larger candles often has wicks on both sides, confirming the market top/bottom and the bull/bear battle.

The abandoned baby/evening star pattern is a reverse pattern with a long history. Price gaps upward after a strong trend but fails to maintain it. The third candle is a powerful move in the other direction, indicating the trend reversal.

The most crucial aspect of this pattern is that you must wait for the third candle to confirm the reversal and the pattern.

- *Doji - Spinning top.*

Dojis are common and go by a variety of names. On the other hand, you can interpret them in a variety of ways, and their true meaning is dependent on the context of your charts.

The body of a Doji candle is often very small, with wicks on both sides. Normally, the wicks are about the same size. Dojis are common after large trend moves and at previous support/resistance levels.

Important aspects and concepts: A Doji by itself is not a signal and should not be traded. A Doji candle is a "warning" candle. Because Dojis can readily occur during sluggish trading sessions, a Doji on the 4H chart is frequently not as relevant, especially in Forex trading.

A Doji is a candle that represents hesitation. A Doji indicates that the market has halted and re-evaluated the situation after a long and robust rally. The size of the wicks on a Doji can frequently reveal a lot about the trade dynamics — long wicks imply a fierce battle between bulls and bears, while little wicks signal passive trading.

When you see a Doji, it's a smart idea to either trail your stop because a reversal is just as likely, or take partial profits to protect yourself from a market turn.

- ***Engulfing or outside bar.***

If it occurs in the correct position and context, the enveloping or outer bar is a strong signal that provides trustworthy signals. The enveloping bar can indicate either a trend reversal or continuance.

A smaller candle is followed by a larger candle that totally engulfs the preceding one in candle formation and sequence. For the best signals, the open AND close of the second, larger candle must usually engulf the preceding one.

Important concepts and characteristics: An engulfing pattern has more meaning when the wicks are little and the second candle is significantly larger than the first. A rejection wick can often be seen at the larger enveloping bar, which strengthens the pattern.

Depending on the direction of the second candle, the engulfing bar might represent a trend reversal or a continuation indicator. Following a sustained rally, a huge red candle can indicate a trend reversal.

However, you can often see engulfing patterns during retracements during trends, and you can utilize this pattern to add to an existing trade or discover a new entry.

The engulfing bar demonstrates great power, with market participants fully reversing price movement. The lower/higher close of the second bar is particularly significant since many traders monitor intraday and daily close/open and use it to make orders.

- **_Inside bar and Fakey._**

The inner bar is similar to the Doji, but it's a fairly common pattern with interesting psychological implications.

The inside bar is the polar opposite of the engulfing pattern in candle creation and succession. The inside bar is a little candle that falls into the previous one fully.

The Fakey occurs when the price breaches the inside bar's high/low and then promptly reverses following the inside bar. As a result, a Fakey might be comparable to a fake breakout pattern or a bear/bull trap, in which price appears to breakout but subsequently reverses.

Concepts and features to consider: The key to trading this pattern is to be patient and wait for the candle after the inside bar. Most novice traders employ pending orders for their inside bars, making them extremely sensitive to squeezes - this is why the Fakey pattern commonly appears after an inside bar.

When trading the inside bar, it's preferable to wait for one candle longer than to enter too soon and be squeezed.

An inside bar denotes a brief respite in trading activity, usually after a long trend or before the start of a new one. There is usually a lot of accumulation and distribution going on during an inside bar, and you can sometimes see explosive moves.

The Fakey is a well-known pattern in which pros take advantage of impatient amateur traders' flaws.

- ***Kangaroo tail, hammer, and pinbar.***

The pin bar is one of the most common, if not THE most popular, candlestick patterns. Although the pin bar stands out and is easy to identify in retrospect, the method by which it is generated can reveal a lot about trading psychology.

A long wick on one side and the candle's body on the opposing side define the pin bar candle structure. Usually, there is no or only a little wick on the side of the body.

Concepts and features to consider: After a protracted trend suggests a reversal, a pinbar can appear. During trends, pinbars are typically seen when traders attempt to reverse the trend direction but are refused - these pin bars are trend continuation indications.

As previously indicated, enveloping bars with a long rejection wick are frequently found, and they appear to be a very strong pin bar.

The wick of a pinball machine sometimes represents the impatience of losing amateur traders. Because they try to foresee market changes, amateurs frequently enter far too early. Professionals are aware of this and quickly reverse pricing, resulting in long wicks on the pin bars.

The Analysis of Candlestick Patterns

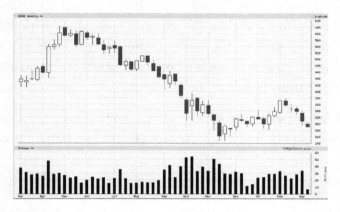

While almost every trader, regardless of experience, can spot the most basic candlestick patterns, certain more advanced patterns require a little more skill to recognize. When correctly read, these patterns can often lead to substantial returns. These patterns frequently involve three or more candlesticks, and they must have extremely precise properties in order to perform properly.

The bearish three-black crow's pattern is an advanced candlestick pattern that traders can exploit. This pattern only appears during a strong upward trend, but a trader may be quite confident that a price reversal is on the way once detected.

This pattern, predictably, is made up of three candlesticks, the first of which must be present near the top of an uptrend. This initial candlestick must have a long body and a lower closing price than the opening price at the same time.

The first crow is said to be that candlestick. On the other hand, the second crow should be identical to the first, except that the opening price should be in the lower half of the first candlestick's body, and the closing price must be lower than the preceding candlestick's.

Finally, the third crow should be the same as the other two, with the exception that it should have the same spatial relationship with the second crow as the second crow does with the first. When the design is finished, it should resemble a series of uniform stairs leading downhill or three black crows gazing down from a tree branch, hence the name.

The three crows are all gazing down, which indicates that lower prices are on the way, and a trader should enter the market now because they can be confident that the market's next trend is negative.

The three white soldiers pattern is another complex pattern that traders can utilize. This configuration looks similar to the three black crows; however, it serves the opposite purpose. Because it indicates a large upward surge in the market, it is known as the three white soldiers.

This pattern only appears near the bottom of a downtrend and has the same appearance as the three black crows, with the exception that the prices of the three candlesticks imply an increase from the opening to the closing price. This forms a pattern that looks like a series of stairs, except instead of going downwards like the three black crows, it's going up. This is a fairly reliable candlestick pattern, similar to the crows, for indicating a significant change in market activity. Traders can rest assured that the slump will come to an end, and the market will turn positive.

The tri-star pattern is another advanced candlestick pattern to consider for traders. This is an unusual but very reliable combination of three Doji stars that appear at the same time. The middle star must be raised above the other two, parallel to each other. A price reversal will occur if this pattern is spotted at the peak of an uptrend, and the market direction will reverse if the opposite pattern is seen at the bottom of a downtrend.

Candlestick Patterns: Advanced Techniques

Price Rejection

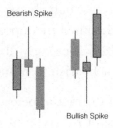

Bearish Spike

Bullish Spike

For hundreds of years, candlestick patterns have been used to forecast and plan everything from rice consumption in Japan to financial assets in the Western world. Candlestick patterns are generally one of the first things traders learn to use because of their long history in business and finance.

However, many traders may not be able to employ these formations successfully if they only have a basic understanding of them. If a trader simply uses basic analytical tools, the trader will lose the benefit of employing the tools in the first place. Instead of relying on the same approaches over and over, you should employ a set of advanced techniques to achieve your goals.

- ***Reversals on an Island.***

The island reversal is the best predictor of a big trend change when looking for strong short-term reversals. The trader must find a gap between a reversal candlestick and two candlesticks on either side. Traders must remember to search for a few specific signs to indicate the occurrence of an island reversal. Identifying entry and departure points will determine whether or not you can correctly forecast what will happen next.

Entry.

The ability to correctly identify an entry point is the first step for traders. An entry point is a fight between bulls and bears, with both sides pushing each other in opposite directions. Typically, the Doji, which resembles a cross, will appear clearly above or plainly below a bullish or bearish trending market.

This gives the island its distinct appearance. When a trader uses candlestick analysis to spot this type of pattern, they know it's a sure sign that a reversal is on the way. Due to the rapidity with which some markets operate, traders may be required to identify an entry that happened in less than five minutes, necessitating the identification of this component of the island reversal.

Exit.

Thankfully, the trader was able to locate the island reversal's entry point. Isn't it now time for them to kick back and relax? Wrong; the trader must constantly examine the circumstance in order to determine when the trend will terminate. When the security trend shows a dramatic reversal, it's time to sell the stock.

- ### *The San Ku Design.*

This pattern, also known as the Three Gaps Pattern, does not imply a trend reversal and should not be followed. Rather, it indicates to the trader that a reversal is imminent.

This reversal can happen with penny stocks that are traded on a daily basis or large corporate equities. Because the pattern appears in every circumstance, it should be noted carefully. The entry and exit points are crucial once again, although they differ slightly from other entry and exit points.

Entry.

The entry is based on the assumption that after a dramatic spike in an asset's price, traders will begin to sell the security quickly in order to profit from the transaction. Other merchants will be able to start their own deals as a result of this.

The item is in reference to the presence of statistically significant increases. Common average tests, such as the MAD (mean absolute deviation equation), can be used to demonstrate this. The security value should not go beyond or below the standard deviations produced by this method. When a stock enters an unusual zone like this, it should be considered for entry.

Exit.

Three gaps will appear again as the exit is approached. You should exit the security when the gaps are closed, and no breakout happens. Traders should be careful of such breakouts in order to protect their positions.

7 Things Beginners Should Know About Candlestick Patterns

1. Because of the numerous Market Participant groups who trade or invest in that market, different markets produce diverse candlestick patterns. Stock, commodity and bond candlesticks will all be different from forex candlesticks. The candlesticks that form on individual equities will be substantially different from those that appear on indexes

and ETFs. This is because indexes are a measure of value rather than a price. The value is determined by formulating and averaging the securities that make up the index or ETF.

2. k created the initial Japanese candlestick designs for the Rice Commodity Exchange in the 1600s. Commodities trading differs from stock trading or trading in any other financial sector. Furthermore, the types of people that traded rice in old Japan were not the same as the Market Participants we have in our current automated marketplace. That means that many of the current candlestick patterns did not exist back then.

3. As our Market Structure evolves and changes, Candlestick Patterns evolve and alter as well. It's crucial to find new patterns that are reliable and constant.

4. It's not just about today's candlestick on the stock chart. It also recognizes the link between recent candlestick formations and previous weeks or months' candlestick formations. The patterns become less dependable and useful as entry signals without a Relational Analysis.

5. Candlestick patterns aren't merely a way to validate a trend or a run. They also define the types of support and resistance, where stop losses should be placed, the proper entry pattern for a particular stock, the trade's run or target gain potential, and the risk versus profit potential. Using candlestick analysis, this information can mean the difference between a highly profitable trade and a series of losses.

6. When it comes to price management, each Market Participant group uses a particular candlestick pattern and trend. This is one of the most useful pieces of information a trader or investor can get from appropriate current candlestick analysis. You can predict

what form of price movement will occur next if you know who controls the price.

7. Current Market Situation Part of the analysis is based on the types of sideways, uptrend, and downtrend candlestick patterns that are forming in a big percentage of the charts. This data is critical for selecting the best buy signals, determining the best trading style, and anticipating the future price action.

Using Candlestick Chart in Equity Trading

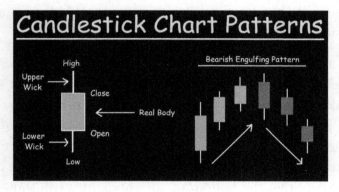

Trading in the financial markets is not for the faint of heart or those who are unfamiliar with technical analysis. Learning about candlestick chart patterns is one approach to improve your chances of making money in the financial markets. Candlestick charts have a lengthy history, with rice dealers in eighteenth-century Japan being claimed to have employed them. When it comes to stock trading, using candlestick charts and looking at the stock's historical trading history can help a stock trader predict what the stock will do in the future.

On a stock chart, each candlestick has its own shape. The body of the candle changes every day depending on whether the stock closed higher or lower for the day.

In most circumstances, if the stock closed up for the day, the candle would be white or light in color, depending on the stock trader's preference. The candle body is also wide, with the upper section of the candle representing the stock's closing price on the day and the lower portion representing the stock's opening price in the trading session. It should be observed that thin lines can be seen emanating from the bottom and top of the candlesticks, but this is not always the case. The shadows are thin lines that illustrate the range in which the stock trades during the day.

When a shadow appears on the top of a white candlestick, it represents the stock's high for the day during the market session. A shadow at the bottom of the candlestick represents the stock's lowest point during the day. When a stock has a down day, the candlestick is usually red or dark, depending on the choice of the stock trader. A down-day candlestick is similar to a white candlestick, except that the bottom of the candlestick will show where the stock finished for the day, while the upper candlestick will reflect where the stock opened for the day.

The length of each day's candlesticks will fluctuate depending on price movement during the trading session. Because purchasing pressure pushed the stock higher, it will show a lengthy white body when it is moving higher. The candlestick portrays the sell-off with a long red or dark candlestick on down days when traders and investors are selling. Long red candlesticks indicate selling pressure, whereas long white candlesticks indicate purchasing pressure.

Short and fat candlesticks indicate that a battle between buyers and sellers was taking place, with no clear winner because the price did not change considerably. A Doji is also known as a candlestick without a body and merely a flat line with shadows on the top and bottom of the straight line. In some circumstances, the Doji shows as the stock undergoes a trend change. The battle that occurred during the trading session is shown by the flat horizontal line with no candlestick body. The high and low points of the session are represented by the shadows at the top and bottom of the horizontal line. When the Doji occurs, the stock may reverse course and move in the opposite direction of the previous trading session.

Learning to read and comprehend candlestick charts may disclose a variety of information about companies, including their past performance and potential future performance. A commander of an army getting news from the front lines of a battle, displaying the daily conflict between his army and the opposing army, is analogous to reading a candlestick chart. The purchasers were in charge on days when the candlestick was long and white. The sellers won the day when the candlestick was lengthy and crimson. The contest was a draw with no clear winner on days when the candlestick was short or non-existent.

Candlesticks and their patterns are significant indicators that can help a trader decide when to enter and exit a stock market. They can also assist in removing emotion from the trading process. Emotion tends to obstruct rational cognition, causing the trader to make rash decisions that result in losses. Every stock trader and investor should have a candlestick charting tool in their toolbox.

Using Candlestick Charts – Stock Market Trading Strategies

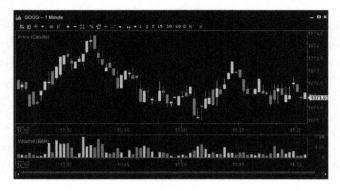

If you want to investigate the possibility of making money through stock trading, you must first have sufficient expertise. Stock trading can bring you money, but you must also understand how to use the tools of the trade.

Candlestick charts, for example, are a simple technique that can be used in stock trading. Candlestick charts can be an excellent and straightforward tool to start with, especially if you are a beginner or new to stock trading.

Candlestick charting has been around for a long time and is one of the greatest tools for novices because it is simple to understand and provides a wealth of information with a single glance. Candlestick charts also allow traders to see trends and prices in a very visual format, and they provide a clear image of the market condition, which aids in decision-making.

The candlestick chart resembles a cross between a line chart and a bar chart, and it depicts market patterns in the stock market. The structure of each bar-line resembles that of a candlestick, which is most likely why it is called such. The candlestick's body reflects the opening and closing transactions, while the line, or wick, symbolizes the highest and lowest transacted values. There are also black and white candlesticks, as well as colored candlesticks that show the direction of the candlesticks.

You must become familiar with various candlestick patterns in order to use candlestick charts and analyze market movements. The Dark Cloud Cover, Doji, Hammer, the Evening Star, Morning Star, Hanging Man, and a slew of other patterns are among the most important to learn. Pattern names that are simple to memorize make this a simple tool for both beginners and experts.

Learning to recognize these patterns allows you to determine whether or not it is beneficial to buy or sell today. Of course, stock market trading is about more than just pricing, demand and supply, and patterns. It's also about the traders' emotional reactions. As a result, if you want to be a good trader, you must master risk management as well as patience and impulse control.

It is critical to learn from experts in addition to understanding how to recognize candlestick patterns. Keep an eye on how they make decisions. Examine the qualities and attitudes that led to their achievement. You must also learn to manage risks and uncertainties and be comfortable dealing with them in order to be successful in trading.

New traders are frequently frustrated when they lose money, and they may not recover quickly. One way to prevent these periods is to invest according to how much money you can afford to lose. Trading stocks is dangerous, and you'll almost certainly lose money at some point, but you can minimize your losses by starting with the amount you're willing to lose. Even if you lose, you can always go back to trading.

Work on becoming more at ease with risks, as this is a key component of investment success.

3

Rules Of Multiple Techniques

M oving Averages and Candlestick Patterns

One of the most basic technical indicators is moving averages. It's a simple but effective tool for analyzing price movement as well as candlestick patterns. Moving averages can help by providing a larger picture or trend background, whereas candlestick patterns focus on the short-term buy/sell balance. As a result, employing candlestick patterns and moving averages can assist you in confirming the trend and making a more accurate prediction.

Moving averages can be used in a variety of ways, including moving average crossover, rainbow approach, and so on. This time, however, the focus will be on the relationship between candlestick patterns and moving averages, as well as how to use them effectively in a trade.

What are the Benefits of Using Moving Averages?

A moving average is a useful tool for calculating an asset's average price over a given time period. It can then show you the market's strength as well as its present trajectory. As fresh bars appear, moving averages will move in lockstep with the prices. As a result, as the price rises, the moving average will rise with it. The same is true if the price drops to a lower level, in which case the moving average will also drop. As a result, the moving average is frequently employed as a base technical analysis that traders can supplement with additional technical indicators to improve prediction accuracy.

The setting

- The Simple Moving Average is a type of moving average (SMA).
- Period of the Moving Average: 30.
- 5-minute Candlestick Chart

The Buy Setup

- Look for a bullish candlestick following a downtrend or range market.
- Check to see if the candlestick breaks below the Moving Average.
- When the High broke through the Moving Average, place a buy entry.

The Sell Setup

- Look for a bearish candlestick following an uptrend or range market.
- Check to see if the candlestick crosses over the Moving Average.
- When the price broke through the Moving Average, place a sell entry at the low of the price.

Oscillators and Candlestick Patterns

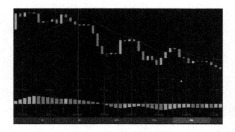

Although candlestick patterns and oscillators can be used separately, combining them will provide you with a better understanding of short-term trading possibilities as well as market direction and momentum. As a result, swing traders who specialize in using technical analysis to profit from short-term price swings would love this combo.

Swing traders search for short-term reversals to profit from future price movements. When the asset changed direction, they would ride the wave in one direction for a while before moving to the opposing side of the transaction.

The first step is to determine the appropriate reversal condition, which can be seen in either candlesticks or oscillators. Indecisive candles or candles that demonstrate a profound shift in sentiment describe candlestick reversals. Reversals in oscillators, on the other hand, can be noticed in the dvergence.

Divergence of the Oscillator

When the price moves in the opposite direction of the indicator, this is known as divergence in oscillators. Consider tossing a ball into the air; it will ultimately lose momentum before reversing direction. Here, too, the same idea applies.

Before the price reverses, momentum slows, and divergence signals that momentum is slowing, indicating that a probable reversal is on the way. Keep in mind that divergence does not signal all reversals, but it does signal the majority of them. Although divergence isn't always required, when it is, candlestick reversal patterns are more likely to be more effective and result in better trades.

The divergence of an oscillator is depicted in the charts below. While the chart's trend is upward, the oscillator displays the exact opposite because the line is moving slower and downward. The divergence suggests trend weakness, which can be confirmed by observing the market activity. The price only managed to reach fresh highs before plummeting. The price eventually reduces dramatically.

Engulfing Patterns: Bullish and Bearish

Engulfing patterns are among the most well-known candlestick patterns available. Bullish and bearish engulfing patterns are the two types of engulfing patterns.

In a decline, a bullish candlestick pattern always appears. The price moves lower, which is often represented by red or black candles. Then there's a big candle, usually green or white in color, that's bigger than the previous bearish candle. The previous down candle must be totally engulfed by the up candle, indicating that substantial purchasing has entered the market. You can begin trading at the bullish engulfing candle's close or near the next open.

The bearish engulfing pattern works in the same way as the bullish engulfing pattern but in the opposite direction. The price should be rising, but the last up candle is enveloped by a massive down candle. This indicates that the sellers are aggressively entering the market.

Indecision Candlesticks

The spinning top pattern is another popular candlestick style. It is made up of a small body with lengthy tails. Because there is volatility during the duration, the pattern shows indecision, but the price is close to where it started by the conclusion of the time. While spinning tops can appear on their own and suggest a trend reversal, they can also appear in groups of two or three. After that, the price will make a significant move in one direction or the other and close in that direction.

The Inverted Hammer Candlestick Pattern: How to Master It

Many candlesticks trend reversal and continuation patterns exist. These candlestick patterns might help you determine whether a trend is reversing or continuing. An important trend reversal pattern, 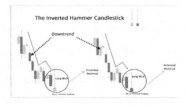 the Inverted Hammer Candlestick Pattern, can accurately identify a trend reversal. This pattern appears infrequently, but when it does, it indicates that the trend will shortly reverse.

The first day of the downturn is marked by a typical bearish candle. On the second day or signal day, you'll notice that the inverted hammer is unusual, as the price movement required to form such a pattern is uncommon.

The bottom of an inverted hammer has a very small body, while the top has a long wick. Because the high is so far above the body, the majority of commerce took place in a tiny area near the low. This low will act as a support in few days.

To trade this bullish inverted hammer pattern, you should wait for confirmation the next day. Assume that the next day's open, following the formation of the inverted hammer pattern, is higher than the previous day's low. The inverted hammer pattern is a real pattern in that instance, and you can trade it by setting your stop loss at the same level as the days open.

The bearish inverted hammer indicates that the uptrend is about to stop and that a downtrend is about to begin. On the first day, you'll see a bullish long white candle, similar to the type that usually occurs in an uptrend. Then there's a gap that opens up, which leads to additional buying at the start.

However, the bears eventually seize control of the market. The bears begin to reduce the prices. The close is the same as or extremely close to the day's low. When you see a bearish inverted hammer, sell or go short by putting your stop near to the second or signal day's open.

As an ambitious trader, though, you can set your stop loss at the height of the inverted hammer produced on the second or signal day. Always stick to the rules. Place your pauses and wait for the market to continue to move. You can make a significant profit if the market swings in the direction you predicted. The stop-loss order will take you out of the trade at a very tiny loss if the future price action does not confirm the candlestick pattern. The price action may retrace at times, but disciplined traders will stick to the principles.

Fibonacci and Candlesticks

You can use candlestick formations in conjunction with another technical analysis tool to determine the best timing to enter or exit a trade. You can use them in conjunction with the Fibonacci Retracement, for example.

The advantage of employing Japanese candlestick forms is that you can obtain the earliest sign of a market direction change. The U-turn is the most typical reversal you may trade.

Charting

Any candlestick, including a Japanese candlestick, can be used to analyze price fluctuations over time. The Candlestick chart is a sophisticated tool that can be used in place of a traditional line or bar chart.

There are over a hundred candlestick formations; however, the important formations are less than ten. The Japanese candlesticks can be recognized in any timeframe (M5, M15, M30, H1, H4, D1, or even longer charts).

Incorporated Data in Candlestick Formations

Candlestick formations are made up of bodies and **wicks that contain four different sorts of data:**

- The starting price
- Closing cost
- Expensive
- Low cost

The body is the candlestick-filled area, while the shadows are the thin lines above and below the body.

Using Fibonacci Retracements in conjunction with Japanese Candlesticks

The Fibonacci retracement can be used in conjunction with a variety of technical analysis indicators, as well as candlestick patterns.

The goal of using the Fibonacci retracement in conjunction with Japanese patterns is to determine trend exhaustion (exhaustive candlesticks). After a powerful bullish or bearish trend, this exhaustion might develop.

How to Use Japanese Candlesticks with Fibonacci Retracement

- The Fibonacci Retracement tool is used after a strong trend has finished and the trend is correcting.
- Fibonacci levels are used to identify likely retracement zones (23.6 percent, 38.2 percent, 61.8 percent, and 78.6 percent).
- We don't trade the reversal unless a reversal candlestick pattern develops when the price reaches a Fibonacci Level.
- Once a position appears, we place a stop-loss order above or below the most recent local high/low.
- The Hammer, Shooting Star, Spinning Top, and Railway Tracks are the most prevalent reversal formations.

Candlestick Trading

What Makes Price Action Signals Effective?

There can be some ambiguity when it comes to price action. Because other traders are trading the same signals as us, we use price action trading signals like the engulfing bar or advanced breakout setups in our members' work. If we trade an engulfing bar on the 4hr chart, for example, we hope that others are also trading the same signal in order for it to be a winner.

This isn't how the market works. You can gain insight into the market's behavior as a price action trader. It doesn't matter what time frame you choose; you'll always be looking at what the market is doing in real-time, right on your chart. The price on your chart represents all of the buyers and sellers in the market at that particular moment. When you examine price action on a chart, all you are doing is observing the behavior of all the traders in the market and what they have done. Humans and traders both react and behave in the same way throughout time. They will never behave in the same way, which is why no approach is, and will never be, completely accurate.

Despite this, traders tend to repeat the same behaviors in comparable situations. There will always be a fantastic possibility to profit from trading price action as long as there are humans in the marketplace. Universal instincts are present in all humans. These impulses are hardwired into our bodies and cannot be modified. Fear of missing out on a deal, fear of losing, greed, peer pressure, and so on are examples of these things.

While these universal tendencies can be controlled, which is why some individuals are able to make money, they DO make mistakes, which is why there will always be a potential to make money as long as humans trade the markets. These errors show up in the price action, and it's in the repeated price action

51

patterns that price action traders can start to profit from. Price action traders aren't simply trading patterns; they're also trading human behavior, order flow indications, and a variety of other market elements.

All of the information is kept by Price. So many traders in the trading market spend hours upon hours looking for fancy indicators, hours upon hours following the news, and thousands of dollars on pricey systems. They'll all be able to locate such information in the price. Traders buying and selling are the only things that change prices up and down. The news has little effect on price movement. Prices are not moved by indicators. Traders trading higher or lower prices is the only thing that changes the price up or down. That's the only option. When a large piece of news is released, it has little effect on stock prices. When something huge occurs on a worldwide scale, such as a major terrorist incident, the stock market does not react.

Why do prices fluctuate? Because merchants speculate on whether the price will rise or fall. The price does not vary in response to news or world events. This is why it is so typical for traders to be watching an announcement and see the price move in the opposite direction of what they expected.

Patterns of a Single Candlestick

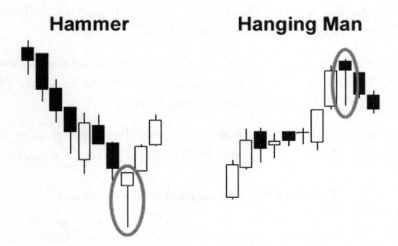

Let's talk about how to distinguish single candlestick patterns now that you're familiar with basic candlestick patterns. These candlesticks can indicate probable market reversals when they appear on a chart. The four fundamental single Japanese candlestick patterns **are as follows:**

Hanging Man and Hammer

The Hammer and the Hanging Man may appear identical, but their implications alter depending on previous price action. Both have adorable small black or white bodies with extended lower shadows and short or no upper shadows.

During a downturn, the Hammer is a bullish reversal pattern. The market is pounding out a bottom, hence the moniker.

Hammers indicate that the bottom is near and that the price will rise again when the price is falling. The extended lower shadow suggests that sellers pushed prices lower, but purchasers fought back and closed close to the open.

You should not automatically put a purchase order just because you see a hammer appear in a downtrend! Before it's safe to pull the trigger, more bullish confirmation is required.

Waiting for a white candlestick to close above the open to the right side of the Hammer is a good example of confirmation.

Criteria for a Hammer's Recognition

- The long shadow is approximately two or three times the size of the original body.
- There is little to no overhead shadow.
- The genuine body is trading at the top of the range.
- It makes no difference what color the real body is.

The Hanging Man is a bearish reversal pattern that can also be used to identify a top or strong resistance level.

The creation of a Hanging Man while the price is rising signals that sellers are beginning to outnumber purchasers.

The extended lower shadow indicates that during the session, sellers pushed prices lower. The price was pushed back up by buyers, but just around the open.

This should raise red flags since it indicates that there are no more buyers available to offer the necessary momentum to continue raising the price.

Criteria for a Hanging Man's Recognition

- A long lower shadow is approximately two or three times the size of the actual body.
- There is little to no overhead shadow.
- The genuine body is trading at the top of the range.

Although a black body is more bearish than a white body, the color of the body is unimportant.

Shooting Star and Inverted Hammer

The Inverted Hammer and Shooting Star have the same appearance. The only difference is whether you're in an upswing or a decline.

- A bullish reversal candlestick is an Inverted Hammer.
- A bearish reversal candlestick is known as a Shooting Star.

Both candlesticks feature small (filled or hollow) bodies, extended top shadows, and little (or non-existent) lower shadows.

Inverted Hammer: When the price has been declining, the Inverted Hammer appears, indicating the chance of a turnaround. Its extended top shadow indicates that bidders attempted to raise the price.

When vendors saw what the buyers were doing, they exclaimed, "Oh hell no!" and attempted to lower the price.

Fortunately, the buyers had consumed enough Wheaties for breakfast and were able to keep the session close to the open. Because the sellers were unable to drop the price any further, it's safe to assume that everyone who wanted to sell has already done so. Who will be left if there are no more sellers? Buyers.

Shooting Star:The Shooting Star is a bearish reversal pattern that resembles the inverted Hammer but happens when the market is rising. Its shape suggests that the price started at the bottom, rebounded, and then fell back to the bottom. This indicates that buyers attempted to raise the price, but sellers intervened and defeated them.

This is a pessimistic sign since there are no more buyers because they have all been overpowered.

Major Candlesticks Reversal Patterns

A candlestick reversal pattern is made up of one to three candlesticks that are arranged in a precise way. They can also signify a potential change in trend direction if you learn to detect them on charts. This is when the tide starts to turn.

The techniques and explanations for the most frequent reversal candlestick patterns can be found below.

- ***Bullish patterns.***

At the end of a downtrend, bullish reversal patterns form, signaling a price turnaround to the upside.

- ***Hammer.***

This is a one-candle pattern. It can indicate the end of a bearish trend, a bottom, or a level of support. The lowest shadow of the candle should be at least twice the length of the true body. It doesn't matter what color the hammer is, but if it's bullish, the signal is greater.

Hammers are a common and easily identifiable sound. They indicate that, while bears were able to push the price to a new low, they were unable to hold it and were defeated by buyers before the end of the trading period. If a hammer forms after a long price decrease, the indication is stronger.

Furthermore, if a hammer is followed by a candlestick that closes above the opening price of the candlestick to its left, the buy signal will be more reliable. **Here's how a hammer sees the actual graph:**

- ***Morning star.***

This is a three-candle pattern. There is a bearish gap down after a long bearish candle. The bears have the upper hand, but they don't do anything. The second candle is relatively small, and its hue is unimportant, albeit a bullish candle is preferable. The third bullish candle has a gap up opening and fills the last bearish gap. This candle is usually a little longer than the first.

Gaps are not required for this pattern, but the reversal signal will be stronger if they are present.

- ***Morning Doji star.***

This is a three-candle pattern. The second candlestick is a Doji, which is nearly identical to the first.

This pattern's signal is deemed stronger than that of a basic "morning star" pattern.

- ***Inverted hammer.***

This is a one-candle pattern. The candle has a small body with a lengthy top shadow that is at least twice as long as the actual body.

It doesn't matter what color the hammer is, but if it's bullish, the signal is greater. A bullish confirmation is always needed after an inverted hammer.

- ***Piercing line.***

This is a two-candle pattern. Long and bearish, the first candlestick. The second candlestick begins with a gap down, below the first's closing level. It's a large bullish candlestick that closes over 50% of the body of the previous candle. Both bodies should be of sufficient length.

The pattern demonstrates that, despite the fact that trading began with a bearish impulse, purchasers were able to reverse the situation and lock in their gains. The signal is strong but not overwhelming.

- ***Bullish harami.***

This is a two-candle pattern. The second candle's body is totally enclosed within the first's body and is the opposite color.

It's worth noting that a harami pattern always necessitates confirmation: the next candlestick must be large and bullish.

- ***Bullish harami cross.***

The harami design is comparable to a two-candle motif. The last day is a Doji, which is the only difference.

You can notice how similar this pattern is to the "morning Doji star" pattern. The rationale and ramifications are the same.

- ***Bullish engulfing pattern.***

At the bottom of the downtrend, a 2-candle pattern forms. Bearish is the first candlestick. The second candlestick should open below the previous candlestick's low and close above it.

As the bullish price action totally engulfs the bearish one, this pattern generates a powerful reversal signal. The stronger the purchase signal, the larger the difference in size between the two candlesticks.

- ***Three white soldiers.***

This is a three-candle pattern. There are three bullish candles with extended bodies in a row. Each candle should light within the preceding body, preferably over the center. Each candle closes at a new peak, close to its highest point.

Although the pattern's dependability is quite high, a confirmation in the form of a white candlestick with a higher close or a gap-up is recommended.

- **_Bearish reversal patterns._**

At the end of an uptrend, bearish reversal patterns form, indicating that the price will most likely fall.

- **_Shooting star._**

This is a one-candle pattern. The body of the candle is quite small. The upper shadow is long and at least twice as long as the body.

The long upper shadow indicates that the market attempted to seek resistance and supply but bears rejected the upward movement. The candle can be any hue, but the signal is greater if it's bearish.

- **_Evening star._**

This is a three-candle pattern. There is a bullish gap up after a long bullish candlestick. The bulls have the upper hand, but they don't do anything. The second candlestick is modest and of no significance in terms of color. The third bearish candle has a gap down opening and fills the last bullish gap. This candle is usually longer than the first.

It's preferable if this pattern has gaps, but it's not a requirement.

- **_Evening Doji star._**

This is a three-candlestick pattern. The pattern is comparable to the "evening star," but it is regarded as a more powerful signal than the middle candle of a Doji.

This pattern's signal is thought to be greater than that of a simple evening star pattern.

- *Hanging man.*

This is a one-candlestick pattern. It can indicate the end of a bullish trend, a peak, or a level of resistance. The lowest shadow of the candle should be at least twice the length of the true body. The candle can be any hue, but the signal is greater if it's bearish.

More bearish confirmation is needed to validate the pattern. When a bearish candlestick closes below the open of the candlestick on the left side of this pattern, the sell signal is confirmed.

- *Dark cloud cover.*

This is a two-candle pattern. The first candle has a long body and is bullish. The second candlestick should open much higher than the first's closing level and close at less than half of the first's body. The sell signal is strong but not overwhelming.

On a chart, **here's an example of this pattern:**

- *Bearish engulfing pattern.*

This is a two-candle pattern. The first candlestick indicates a bullish trend. The second candlestick is bearish, and it should open above the high of the first candlestick and close below it.

As the bearish price action totally engulfs the bullish one, this pattern generates a powerful reversal signal. The stronger the sell signal, the larger the difference in size between the two candlesticks.

- ***Bearish harami.***

This is a two-candle pattern. The second candle's body is totally enclosed within the first's body and is the opposite color.

Always remember that harami patterns need confirmation: the next candlestick should be large and bearish.

- ***Bearish harami cross.***

Harami is a motif made up of two candlesticks. The second candlestick is a Doji, which distinguishes it from the first.

- ***Three black crows.***

This is a three-candlestick pattern. There are three bearish candles with extended bodies in a row. Each candle burns within the preceding one's body, ideally below its middle. Each candle closes at a new low, close to its lowest point.

Although the pattern's dependability is very strong, a confirmation in the form of a bearish candlestick with a lower closure or a gap-down is recommended.

Candlestick Patterns That Are Most Profitable and Proven

Candlestick pattern (or formation) is a technical analysis term used to depict the price patterns of a security or asset in the forex, stock, commodities, and other markets. Candlestick charts are simple to interpret and provide advance warnings of market turning points.

Candlestick charts depict market movements and provide insight into the underlying causes that support the trend.

The candlestick charts assist in determining market entry and exit points. By applying candlestick technical analysis and being in the correct position at the appropriate time, the trader might potentially reduce risk exposure.

Japanese candlestick charts are another name for candlestick charts. Candlestick charts can be utilized for all trading methods, including day trading, swing trading, and long-term position trading, and can be used on all time frames.

Candlestick patterns are separated into two categories: bullish patterns and bearish patterns. Candlestick patterns are constructed with the use of one or more candles, and they signify trend reversal or continuation of a long-term trend.

The most common candlestick patterns employed by forex traders to analyze market conditions **are as follows:**

Engulfing Candlesticks Pattern

Direction: Bullish and bearish

Bullish or bearish reversal patterns are engulfing candlestick patterns. Two candlesticks make up the engulfing candlestick patterns. Bullish engulfing candlestick patterns are most common when the market is in decline. The tiny candlestick is being engulfed by the huge green candlestick. This pattern signals the end of a bearish move/downtrend and the start of a bullish trend in the case of an asset. In practice, the enveloping pattern can also be referred to as the outside bar pattern.

The bearish engulfing pattern, in which the huge red/black candle engulfs the white/green candle, shows the inverse signal of the bullish engulfing pattern. It usually shows up during an upsurge. The pattern indicates that the trend is continuing and that the price is higher than the previous day's close, but that the price eventually closes lower than the previous day's opening or low.

Hammer Candlestick Pattern

Direction: Bullish

The bullish candlestick reversal pattern is known as the hammer. As depicted in the image, the candle resembles a hammer, with a long lower shadow and a short body, and no or a very short upper shadow. A solitary candle makes up the hammered pattern.

When the asset's price declines during a downtrend, the hammer appears, signifying the end of the bearish trend.

When the asset price falls from its opening price during a trading session, the hammer candlestick pattern develops, and the closing price ends near the opening price following recovery. It makes little difference whether the hammer's body is bullish or bearish in this case. In practice, the hammer pattern is also known as the bullish Pin Bar pattern.

Harami Candlestick Pattern

Direction: Bullish and bearish

A long black/red body candle is followed by a tiny white/green body candle in the bullish harami pattern. The market is currently in a negative trend, as evidenced by the red candle, but the price is trading higher the next day. These patterns could indicate the end of a long-term negative trend or a trend reversal.

In bearish harami patterns, a little black/red candle follows a large white/green candle. The pattern implies that the bullish trend is reversing.

The harami candlestick pattern is commonly referred to as the inside bar pattern.

Piercing Candlestick Pattern

Direction: bullish or bearish

Two candlesticks make up this motif. The reversal pattern for a bullish piercing is a black or red candle followed by a white or green candle that starts lower with a down gap (which is unusual in currencies) and closes out more than half of the previous candle's range.

As the asset price downtrends and begins to move upward, the piercing pattern denotes the reversal of the bearish trend.

Bearish piercing candlestick patterns appear to be the polar opposite.

Doji Candlestick Pattern

Direction: bullish or bearish

The Doji symbol suggests that the market is resting. The underlying asset's price closes fairly close to its opening price. The lack of a physical body suggests that market participants, such as sellers and buyers, are unable to overcome one another, resulting in price stagnation during the trading period. It could be interpreted as a continuation pattern of the long-term trend or as an indication of a reversal pattern of current market movements.

Shooting Stars Candlestick Pattern

Direction: bearish

The shooting star design resembles a hammer inverted. During an uptrend, a shooting star is a bearish reversal candlestick pattern. Although the price is rising, it appears that the bullish trend is continuing, but the candle closes near the opening price, indicating a possible reversal.

The Basic Type of Candlestick

Marubozu

Marubozu Full	Marubozu Open	Marubozu Close

bullish	bearish	bullish	bearish	bullish	bearish

In Japanese, Marubozu means "bald head" or "shaved head," which reflects the candlestick's lack of shadows.

The absence of shadows on a Marubozu candlestick indicates that the session began at the highest price and ended at the lowest price of the day.

A Marubozu is a Japanese candlestick that is long or tall and has no above or bottom shadow (or wick).

The extended body of the candlestick pattern makes it easier to recognize in both bearish (red or black) and bullish (green or white) forms.

It has the appearance of a vertical rectangle.

Look for the following characteristics when identifying a Marubozu **candlestick pattern:**

- The body of the solitary candle used in the signal should be long.
- There should be no upper or lower shadows (or wick).
- The candle can be white/green, black/red, or any color in between, and it can appear anywhere on the chart.
- A white/green Marubozu is particularly bullish and moves upward.
- A black/red Marubozu is bearish and travels downward.
- The stronger the price change, the longer the candle is.

A White Marubozu is a bullish Marubozu, whereas a Black Marubozu is a bearish Marubozu.

The purchasers controlled the price throughout the session in a bullish Marubozu, from start to finish.

The sellers controlled the price from the open to the close in a bearish Marubozu. To better analyze a specific Marubozu, **observe the following:**

- If a White Marubozu appears near the end of an uptrend, expect it to continue.
- A reversal is likely if a White Marubozu appears at the end of a downtrend.
- A continuation is expected if a Black Marubozu happens at the end of a decline.
- A reversal is likely if a Black Marubozu appears near the end of an upswing.

Doji

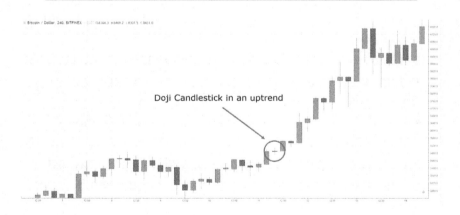

The Doji's form represents a buyer's and seller's uncertainty. When you notice a Doji candlestick pattern, you know the session ended very close to where it began, which is why the candle has no body.

A Doji is a single candlestick pattern that occurs when the starting and closing prices are both the same.

The lack of a physical form implies indecision or a tug-of-war between buyers and sellers, and the power dynamic may be altering.

The length of the top and lower shadows might differ, giving the candlestick a cross, inverted cross, or plus sign appearance.

The Doji is normally thought of as a neutral pattern on its own, but it is frequently used in multi-candlestick patterns.

The Doji is the tiniest and most basic of all candlesticks, making it extremely easy to spot. **Keep the following parameters in mind:**

- The candlestick's open and close must be at (or near) the same price level, or the Doji will lack a body or have a very small body.
- An upper shadow, a lower shadow, or both must be present.

The Doji's horizontal line indicates that the open and close were at the same level.

Doji's vertical line indicates the timeframe's overall trading range.

Because neither the buyers nor the sellers have power, indecision reigns. There is a tug-of-war going on in which neither party has the upper hand. Despite the fact that the price varied throughout the session, it eventually returned to its original opening price. This period of hesitation frequently precedes a trend reversal.

If the market is not trending, a Doji is less meaningful, as sideways or choppy markets imply indecision.

When a Doji appears in an uptrend, it is usually taken seriously since it indicates that the purchasers are losing faith.

When a Doji appears in a downturn, it is usually taken seriously since it indicates that the sellers are losing faith.

Doji's Gravestone

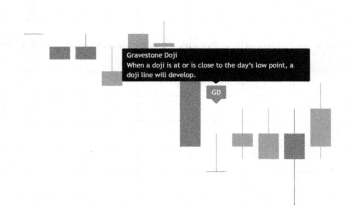

The Gravestone Doji is a Japanese candlestick in which the open and close prices are at or very close to the same level.

Meaning: The Gravestone Doji is a bearish indicator.

A Gravestone Doji indicates that the price opened at the session's low. During the session, there was a strong increase, and then the price fell to the session's low.

As a result, the open, low, and close prices are all the same (or almost so). A Doji candle that opens at or near its low and closes at or near its high. The candle ends up with no body and a long top shadow.

If the top shadow is long, it indicates a bearish reversal. It is considered a reversal indicator when it emerges at the top of an uptrend.

This is a more bearish pattern than a shooting star.

Look for the following characteristics to identify **a Gravestone Doji:**

- The Gravestone Doji is an upside-down capital letter with a long upper shadow but no below shadow.

Consider how an actual gravestone is attached to the earth to help you remember. The Gravestone pattern's horizontal line is fixed at the bottom.

This differs from the Dragonfly Doji, which has a fixed horizontal line at the top.

The appearance of this candlestick pattern is most notable when it occurs after an uptrend and is preceded by bullish candlesticks. It could indicate that the rise is coming to an end.

Dojis are trend reversal indicators, particularly when they arise following an uptrend or decline. A basic Doji denotes indecision, whereas a Gravestone Doji denotes a market choice to be bearish.

A trend reversal is likely to occur when a Gravestone Doji candlestick appears after a strong upswing.

A simple method can open a short position below the Doji's low once you've identified a Gravestone Doji.

Your trade should only be activated when the Doji's low breaks down. The price may restart its upward trend if the Gravestone Doji's low holds.

Doji Dragonfly

The Dragonfly Doji is a bullish indicator.

A Dragonfly Doji indicates that the price opened at the session's high. During the session, there was a significant drop in price, and then the price closed at the session's high.

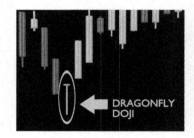

As a result, the open, high, and close prices are all the same (or almost so). When the high, open, and close prices are identical, a single Japanese candlestick pattern known as a Dragonfly Doji is produced.

- It could be an indication of a reversal.
- The candle ends up with no body and a long lower shadow.
- It's most common at the bottom of a downward trend.

A hammer is more bearish than a Dragonfly Doji.

Look for the following characteristics **to identify a Dragonfly Doji:**

- The Dragonfly has a lengthy lower shadow but no upper shadow and looks like a capital T.
- The candlestick is formed when the session's starting and closing prices are at their highest.

When this candlestick emerges after a downtrend and is preceded by bearish candlesticks, it is especially notable. It may indicate that the decline is coming to an end.

Spinning Top

Consider a spinning top when considering the Spinning Top candlestick pattern. When it's spinning smoothly, you have no idea when it'll stop and which way it'll fall.

A Spinning Top candlestick pattern, on the other hand, denotes hesitation.

Neither the buyers nor the sellers had any influence over the situation.

The market did not alter much when it closed versus when it started, as evidenced in the short body of the candlestick.

However, at one point during the session, both the buyers and sellers had the upper hand, as evidenced by the extended upper and lower shadows.

A Japanese candlestick with a small actual body and extended upper and lower shadows is known as a Spinning Top.

The small body of the candle indicates that the market was undecided about the price direction. However, the long shadows show that both buyers and sellers were active during the session. Childen's spinning tops inspired the name of the Spinning Top candlestick pattern.

A Spinning Top features a short body (black or white) and two lengthy shadows, similar to its toy version. Shadows come in a variety of sizes. Indecision is signaled by spinning tops. The less direct the market is, the smaller the body.

A Spinning Top is a neutral pattern that develops significance when combined with other candlestick forms.

The Spinning Top resembles the Doji in appearance. A single candlestick with a long wick extending from the top to the bottom appears in both styles.

Because one has a body (the Spinning Top) and the other has not, it's easy to tell them apart (the Doji). Look for a single candlestick with a short body between two lengthy shadows when finding a Spinning Top candlestick pattern. The hue of one's skin is unimportant.

Spinning The bodies of top candlesticks are typically small, with upper and lower shadows that extend beyond the length of the body.

It's difficult to predict where the market will go next due to this hesitation and uncertainty. A Spinning Top can emerge both up and down because it is neither bearish nor bullish but rather neutral. After an upswing or a downtrend, a Spinning Top may indicate a potential reversal.

The uptrend (downtrend) is stalled for a moment of hesitation (indicated by the Spinning Top), and that lost momentum could signal that the current trend has come to an end.

Spinning Tops frequently appear in charts; however, they are unreliable on their own. They should combine them with other types of technical analysis, such as support and resistance, to get the best results.

4

Bullish Belt Hold Definition

A bullish belt hold is a candlestick pattern that appears in a downtrend and indicates that the current bearish trend may be coming to an end. The bullish belt hold is made up of two candles, the first of which is negative and the second of which gapes down while still closing around the preceding bar's close.

Let's take a closer look at the bullish belt hold and what it means in this part. You'll also learn how to eliminate erroneous trades, which will come in handy if you wish to trade the pattern live.

A bullish belt hold consists of both a bullish and a bearish candle. **The following are the specifics:**

1. The market is in a bearish candle and is in a downturn.
2. The market drops the next day dramatically, but it still manages to close around the previous bar's closing.

The bullish belt hold is commonly interpreted as indicating an impending trend reversal.

What Does the Market Say About a Bullish Belt Hold?

Every candlestick pattern has its own story to tell about the market factors that caused it to form. And, as traders, we can gain a lot by figuring out what pushed the market to where it is now.

Of course, pinpointing the specific reason for a market's behavior is nearly impossible. With that in mind, we can make some educated guesses.

Let's take a look at what the market did while forming a bullish belt hold!

Market sentiment is overwhelmingly negative as the market emerges from a bearish trend, and most people expect prices to fall. As a result, the bullish belt hold pattern's initial bearish candle is formed. The pessimistic attitude remains strong at the following open, causing the market to gap down significantly.

Because the market has become oversold, buyers see an opportunity to get in at a low price and close the gap. The market's fast recovery indicates that buyers have taken control and are likely to push the market higher into a positive trend.

How to Trade the Bullish Belt Hold

You might think that all you have to do now is search for a bullish belt hold and enter a trade as soon as you see one.

It's not that simple, though.

Candlestick patterns are rarely profitable enough to be used solely on their own. Most of the time, you'll need to add filters or conditions to make them worthwhile.

What works well varies a lot depending on the market and duration you trade. This is why we propose doing backtesting to figure out what works and what doesn't.

Entry Postponement

It's possible that a candlestick pattern or other form of signal isn't followed by a price change right away, but only after some time has elapsed.

A bullish belt hold, for example, could indicate a trend reversal that occurs on average 10 bars after the pattern is formed. Perhaps the market will continue to fall for a while before turning around.

It would be prudent for us to wait a while before entering a transaction in such circumstances. We could also watch where the market went soon after the bullish belt hold while we waited.

We might even discover that there is only an advantage when the market continues to fall and that acting on a pattern that is followed by an ascending market only results in losses!

So, in a nutshell, postponing the entrance also gives you the time to confirm the signal.

Using Sentiment Indicators or Market Breadth

If you want a trustworthy signal, it's not always enough to base your research on the price of a single asset. So, what other marketplaces or data sources do you think you could include?

Market sentiment indicators, for example, are a valuable source of information.

Unlike an indicator that is applied to specific securities, a market sentiment indicator assesses the status of the market by looking at a broader set of indicators. Market sentiment indicators, for example, keep track of how many stocks are rising and falling in a certain market. The statistics you acquire from indicators like these can then be used to see if the overall market state backs up your research on a specific market level.

If you see a bullish belt hold and most stocks are down on a given day, it can be an excellent time to buy. At the moment, the stock you're looking at was outperforming the market!

Of course, it's also possible that it's the other way around. This is yet another reason to employ backtesting.

Calculate the Current Trend's Length

Because a bullish belt hold is thought to occur near the end of a bearish trend, the duration of the previous market trends may be important.

For example, if the average length of a trend in your market and timeframe is 50 bars, and the present bearish trend has lasted 60 bars, you may be more confident in a trade.

So, how do you figure out how long a pattern has been going on?

So you go back in time and measure the distance between market peaks and bottoms. Then you use the average of the last 5 or so as a reference!

Just keep in mind that trends can endure a long time and that no strategy is bulletproof!

Trading Strategies for a Bullish Belt Hold

It's time to look at some trading ideas now that we've covered a handful of ways to improve the accuracy of a bullish belt hold pattern.

Keep in mind that none of the trading techniques listed below have been properly backtested and confirmed. They're included for inspiration and to demonstrate that a trading strategy doesn't have to be complicated. The majority of trading strategies are straightforward and effective.

Let's take a look at them now!

1. Bullish Belt Hold in a Gap Situation

One of the major components of the bullish belt hold pattern is the gap between the first and second candles. As a result, it would be worthwhile to give it more attention!

If the pattern has a large gap, for example, buying pressure must be higher to cover it. And, as a result, there's a good likelihood that the market's buying pressure is strong enough to start a new trend!

So, what size should the gap be?

The Average True Range indicator, which smooths out outliers, is one of the better ways to assess range. A moving average of the real range is the Average True Range.

To go long in the market, we may need a gap that is larger than the genuine average range. As a result, **the strategy's rules are that we buy if:**

1. A bullish belt is in place.
2. The difference exceeds the genuine average range.

Then, after 5 bars, we leave the trade!

2. Moving Average Distance Filter With Bullish Belt Hold

We might wish to have a filter that reflects the fact that a bullish belt hold can happen in a downtrend. Moving averages are one of the most common strategies to identify whether a market is bullish or bearish.

When the market falls below the moving average, it is bearish, and vice versa. We could trade if the bullish belt hold was below its moving average if we applied the moving average.

However, we'll take it a step further in this strategy example. The close must be lower than the moving average minus the true average range multiplied by 5.

As a result, the rules for this approach are as follows: **we go long if:**

1. A bullish belt is in place.
2. The market is trading five times the typical real range or more below its 200-period moving average.

When the market closes above the moving average, we exit.

82

5

Identifying
Continuation Patterns

A continuation pattern is a halt or retreat in an established trend that, when finished, should continue to move price in the trend's direction, according to candlestick aficionados. There are a few considerations to bear in mind with continuation patterns, **just as there are with reversal patterns:**

- A continuation pattern isn't a guarantee that the preceding trend will continue; rather, it's an indication that the trend's stop is just short.
- Continuation patterns that appear in a range are not always correct. They are usually preceded by a trend, either upward or downward.
- The majority of continuation patterns have certain requirements. According to tech traders, the closer a pattern is to these parameters, the more probable it is to come out as planned.

Let's take a look at several popular candlestick continuation patterns with that in mind.

Three White Soldiers

The name of this design comes from a time when charts were hand-drawn on paper. Up candles were white and down candles were black in that setting. Up candles are usually green and down candles are red in today's computerized charting.

This pattern consists of three white (green) candles lined up in a row, **with the following criteria:**

- Each of the three candles is lengthy and bearish.
- The opening price of each candle is contained within the body of the previous candle.
- The closing price of each candle is higher than the previous candle.

The location of this pattern determines its kind. It could be a reversal pattern if it happens after a lengthy downturn. If it occurs after a modest retreat in the middle of an existing trend, it is considered a continuation pattern.

Rising Three Methods

The rising three techniques is a bullish continuation pattern that consists of five candles, **despite its name implying three:**

- The first candle is long and bullish, indicating that the uptrend is continuing.
- The next three candles are modest and represent a short-term pullback, all of which close within the body of the first candle.
- The fifth candle is long and bullish, with a higher closing price than the first one.

There may be more than three short candles in this pattern on rare occasions, but it is considered more potent when there are only three.

Separating Lines

Depending on the prior trend direction, this is a two-candle continuation pattern that can be bullish or bearish.

The bullish version is distinguished by the **following characteristics:**

- During an uptrend, the first candle is long and bearish.
- The second candle is lengthy and bullish, with an opening price that is the same as the first.
- There is no lower shadow ("wick") on the second candle.

The qualities of a bearish separating lines pattern are the polar opposite.

In Neck

One of the few continuation patterns that can only be bearish is this last candlestick **pattern:**

- The first candle is long and bearish, indicating that the market is in a downward trend.
- The bullish second candle opens at a new low price.
- The close price of the second candle is equal to or slightly higher than the first candle's close price.

This pattern has a slightly different variation known as on the neck. It, too, indicates only bearish continuation, with the exception that the second candle's closing price is equal to the previous candle's low price.

Bullish Continuation Patterns

Bullish continuation patterns arise in the middle of an uptrend and are easy to spot.

Below are the most important bullish continuation patterns.

- ***Ascending triangle.***

An ascending triangle pattern is a consolidation pattern that appears in the middle of a trend and usually indicates that the trend will continue. As price temporarily moves in a sideways direction, two converging trendlines (flat upper trendline and rising lower trendline) are drawn. Traders look for a subsequent breakout, in the direction of the preceding trend, as a cue to enter a trade.

- ***Bullish Pennant.***

A bullish pennant pattern is a chart pattern that develops when security has seen a large, abrupt upward surge. During a brief period of consolidation, it appears before the price resumes its direction with the same initial impetus.

A Pennant is a triangular pattern made up of many forex candlesticks that are not to be confused with the larger, symmetrical triangle pattern.

- ***Bullish Flag.***

The bullish flag pattern is an excellent pattern to learn for traders. The bull flag is frequently connected with explosive moves because it provides a brief reprieve from a rapid first move. The bull flag and pennant patterns both arise when there is a strong and quick price movement; however, the bull flag can provide more appealing entry levels.

A downward sloping channel marked by two parallel trendlines against the preceding trend defines the bull flag.

- ***Bullish Rectangle pattern.***

The rectangle pattern denotes a trend halt in which price travels sideways between two parallel support and resistance zones. The pattern indicates a price consolidation before continuing in the existing trend's original path. This pattern has the added benefit of allowing traders to trade either within the range or on the final breakout, or both.

Patterns For Bearish Continuation Candlesticks

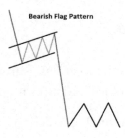

Bearish Flag Pattern

Bearish continuation patterns arise in the middle of a downtrend and are easy to spot. The bearish variants of the above-mentioned comparable patterns have the same effect as the bullish counterparts but in the opposite direction. **Below are the most important bearish continuation patterns.**

- *Descending Triangle.*

The descending triangle pattern is a consolidation pattern that appears in the middle of a trend and usually indicates that the downtrend will continue. As price temporarily moves in a side-ways direction, two converging trendlines (descending upper trendline and flat lower trendline) are drawn. Traders use a subsequent breakout in the direction of the previous trend as a benchmark for entering a trade.

- *Bearish Pennant.*

The bearish pennant is a chart pattern that develops following a substantial, rapid drop in a security's price. During a brief time of consolidation, it appears before the price continues to fall in the direction of the main trend.

- *A Bearish Signal.*

Like the bullish flag, the bearish flag is frequently connected with explosive moves both before and after it appears.

An upward sloping channel marked by two parallel trendlines slanting against the preceding trend defines the bear flag. The rectangle pattern is not to be confused with the flag. The flag takes substantially less time (one to three weeks) to make than the rectangle pattern and has a discernible gradient.

- **_Bearish Rectangle._**

The bearish rectangle pattern denotes a trend pause in which price moves sideways between parallel support and resistance zones. The pattern indicates a price consolidation before continuing in the existing trend's original path. Traders might choose to trade within the range, trade the eventual breakout, or trade both.

Patterns of Trading Continuation

Continuation patterns can be good predictors of future market movement if traders **follow these guidelines:**

1. Determine the trend's direction before the price begins to consolidate.
2. Use trendlines to determine which continuation pattern is likely to emerge.
3. Once the continuation pattern has been identified, set appropriate stops and limits while maintaining a good risk-to-reward ratio.
4. Before joining, traders can wait for a strong breakout in the trend's direction. Traders could also consider using a tight stop to defend against a false breakout and trailing this stop if the market moves in their favor. This, as well as other risk management measures, should be considered.

Continuation Patterns' Advantages

The continuation patterns aid in the organization of our trade. After the momentary break, you may rest assured that the price movement will continue in the same direction. The continuation pattern, on the other hand, assists us in determining the exact entry, take profit, and stop loss. The breakthrough should be stronger than the trend that preceded the pause.

It's also worth noting that not all continuation patterns will result in the same trend continuing. In trading, nothing is guaranteed, and you will see numerous patterns that appear to be continuations but wind-up being reversal formations. Our pattern was in draft mode and never activated if the trend reversed and broke out of the consolidation phase without a breakout in the same direction as the overall trend.

As a result, the failure to advance in the same direction is also one of these patterns' main flaws. As a result, it's critical to check additional technical indicators to ensure that numerous sources are showing that the trend is likely to continue in the near future.

Indecision candlestick patterns

The 'Indecision Candle' is one of the strongest candlesticks signals used in the price action trading technique. In this section, I'll explain what an Indecision candle is and why it's a valuable tool to have in your price action technical trading toolbox.

Other common names are "Doji" and "spinning top," which you may have heard or seen. While there are several criteria that determine how the setup should look, we've consolidated them into a less complex, generic signal known as the 'indecision candle.' The reason for this is that the Doji and the spinning top are structurally quite similar.

The Indecision Candle's Anatomy

The candle must have a small body to qualify (the close price of the candle must be close to the open price). Second, the body of the candle must be at the middle of the candle range (between the high and the low). Finally, the indecision candle must have long, equal-length wicks extending from each side of the body.

The wicks extending from each side of the candle signal to the trader that the price has attempted to move up and down during that candlestick trading session. The market's inability to maintain higher or lower prices is what gives this candlestick pattern its unique anatomy. The telltale indicators of this up and down movement are the wicks jutting out on either side of the candle body.

So, what does this mean? It tells us as price action traders that the bulls and bears were fighting each other throughout the session. The market ends roughly in the same area as its open price because there was no clear winner by the end of the candle's session. The name "indecision candle" comes from this type of action, which displays indecisiveness.

Now that we've grasped this, let's put it to good use! Indecisive candles are great price reversal indicators. After long moves, those that form at key regions on the chart might alert traders to a likely trend reversal or even herald the end of a counter-trend retracement.

At the tops and bottoms of trends, hesitation candles are common. They form when price hits a big reversal area on the chart, such as weekly support or resistance, and orders flood the market as money changes hands.

The massive sums of money being exchanged between the bulls and bears cause the 'whipping' up and down action, which builds the indecisive candle structure, thanks to the high order volume (the upper and lower wicks). The longer the accumulation, the stronger the breakouts are, according to the general rule.

The bulls drove the price up the chart until it reached a high resistance level, at which point the selling intervened. A rush of orders floods the market as buyers and sellers compete for dominance at the key price level.

The resistance level eventually held, and price action traders were able to position themselves for a negative breakout before it occurred. This is why indecision candles are a must-have for every serious price action trader, and they complement swing trading systems beautifully.

Indecision candles are useful not only for reversal signals but also for price continuation signs. Remember that the hesitation candle structure symbolizes market uncertainty, and indecisive price behavior halts market price movement. When the market determines which direction it wants to go when it starts moving again, one of the advantages of price action trading is that you can catch the breakout.

The breakout could be on the other end of the spectrum, as in the case of the usual Indecision candle reversal indication depicted in the example above, or the price could continue advancing in the trend's direction.

As you can see, this hesitation candle presented an excellent opportunity for the trader to profit from the bullish trending market. You can now see how effective the Indecision candle can be when traded properly.

However, be cautious; hesitation candlesticks will appear all over the charts. Regrettably, not every one of them represents a viable trade opportunity. When picking a trade, be cautious. Make sure you can back up your transaction with logic and that you know how to enter a forex trading appropriately.

Types of Indecisive Patterns

In general, there are two types of indecisive patterns that you may encounter over your forex trading career. **These are the patterns:**

1. The Spinning Top Pattern

Spinning. When the market's selling and buying pressures battle it out to bring the price up or down to take control, top indecisive patterns emerge.

Only two things are depicted in this design. One is the ferocious bidding war between buyers and sellers. Another thing it shows is that no one has been able to seize control of the market.

To put it another way, traders utilize the Spinning Top pattern to gauge market volatility. Because it is an indecisive pattern, it cannot reveal who was the market's deciding power in the end.

One of the best things about this pattern is that you don't have to put much effort into it because it's simple to recognize and read.

2. Candlestick Pattern (Doji)

The Doji pattern, like the Spinning Top, is an indecisive candlestick formation that signifies market indecisiveness.

This pattern is nearly typically related to reversals of existing price trends because it forms either at the bottom or at the top of the trend. It can, however, signal trend continuations from time to time.

Dojis are formed when the opening and closing prices reach a point of balance. This happens when bulls try to push prices higher, but bears reject them and try to decrease them.

The bulls eventually fail to keep prices at their desired levels, allowing all bulls on the market to drive prices higher. This back-and-forth movement offers the ideal environment for the formation of a Doji pattern.

There are two major variations of the Doji pattern that you should **be familiar with:**

- **Gravestone Doji:** This pattern is formed when bulls successfully push the price upward.
- **Dragonfly Doji:** This pattern appears when a trend reversal is possible.

How to Trade the Doji Pattern

The Doji pattern comes in a variety of variations that you can study and refer to whenever you see it. Knowing what they are and what they signify can aid you in making accurate trading forecasts.

This basically indicates that you can trade this pattern in a few different ways. The crucial point is always to use an indicator or oscillator to corroborate the pattern's prediction.

Typically, a single Doji's appearance is regarded as a universal indicator of market hesitation. There have been instances where two Dojis appeared next to each other. This signal is interpreted as indicating a significant breakout.

How to Trade the Spinning Top Pattern

Traders should wait for confirmation before entering a trade once the Spinning Top has formed.

When employing technical indicators or oscillators, obtaining positive or negative confirmation signals is simple.

Traders often obtain confirmation of the Spinning Top pattern when the subsequent candlesticks appear, which commonly form at positions such as the point below the Spinning Top's wick.

To summarize, you should trade the candle that has a short body and long wicks on both sides. You can also use trend lines and other indicators to gain a sense of the market's direction.

Always wait for confirmation before starting a trade as soon as you have proof, trade in the direction that is certain to make you money.

Indecisive candlestick patterns can be used as a hint to sit on the sidelines and wait for better opportunities to trade on the foreign exchange market.

Its perseverance and patience will bring you profits. Learning how to keep your money safe and only spend what you need will go a long way toward ensuring your continued participation in the game.

When employing indecisive candles, one thing to keep in mind is that you may end up with a lot of them on your charts, and not all of them will be suitable for trading.

6

Two-Pattern Candle

This chapter delves into two candle patterns, including Bullish and Bearish Engulfing, Piercing Line, and Dark Cloud Cover, as well as how to recognize and use them.

What is an Engulfing Candlestick?

Engulfing candles usually indicate a reversal of the market's current trend. Two candles are used in this pattern, with the second candle enveloping the full body of the candle preceding it. Depending on how it forms in relation to the current trend, the engulfing candle can be bullish or bearish.

Forex Engulfing Patterns Types

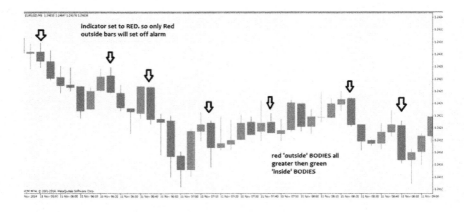

The bullish engulfing candle pattern and the bearish engulfing candle pattern are the two types of engulfing candle patterns.

- *Bullish engulfing pattern.*

When appearing at the bottom of a downtrend, the bullish engulfing candle delivers the greatest indication, indicating a spike in buying pressure. As more buyers enter the market and force prices higher, the bullish engulfing pattern frequently reverses an established trend. The pattern consists of two candles, the second of which entirely engulfs the previous red candle's body.

When the bullish pattern occurs, the price movement must demonstrate a clear downturn. The massive bullish candle indicates that buyers are actively coming in, setting the stage for additional upward momentum. Traders will then use indicators, important levels of support and resistance, and following price action after the engulfing pattern to confirm that the trend is truly turning around.

- *Bearish engulfing pattern.*

The bullish engulfing pattern is the polar opposite of the bearish engulfing pattern. When it appears at the top of an uptrend, it sends out the strongest signal, indicating an increase in selling pressure. As more sellers enter the market and drive prices down, the bearish engulfing candle generally signals a reversal of an established trend. The pattern consists of two candles, the second of which entirely engulfs the previous green candle's body.

When the bearish pattern occurs, the price action must demonstrate a firm increase. The huge bearish candle indicates that sellers are actively piling in, setting the stage for further negative momentum. Traders will then use indicators, levels of support and resistance, and following price action after the engulfing pattern to confirm that the trend is truly turning around.

Why are Engulfing Candles Important for Traders?

Engulfing candles can help traders notice reversals, signify a growing trend, **and provide an exit signal:**

1. Reversals: Recognizing reversals is self-explanatory; it allows a trader to enter a transaction at the best possible price and ride the trend to its conclusion.

2. Trend continuation: Traders can use the engulfing pattern to confirm that the current trend will continue. Seeing a bullish engulfing pattern during an uptrend, for example, gives you more confidence that the trend will continue.

3. Quit strategy: If the trader is holding a position in an existing trend that is coming to an end, the pattern can also be used as a signal to exit an existing trade.

When the pattern becomes more of a retracement than a clear change in direction, the engulfing candle can become limited. Traders might still seek for following price activity to lessen the chances of this unfavorable outcome.

Engulfing Candle Trading Strategies

The Engulfing Candle Reversal Strategy is a strategy for reversing a candle that has been engulfed.

Traders can trade the bearish engulfing pattern by analyzing subsequent price movement for confirmation or waiting for a downturn before entering a trade.

1. Look for a successful closing below the bearish engulfing candle's low to enter. Traders can also wait for a brief retracement (towards the dotted line) before opening a short position.

2. Stop: Stops can be put above the swing high, which is where the bearish engulfing pattern occurs.

3. Set the target/take profit level at a previous level of support while maintaining a positive risk-to-reward ratio. The green and red rectangles represent the risk-to-reward ratio.

When Trend Trading, Use the Engulfing Candle

Engulfing candles don't have to appear at the end of a trend to be effective.

Traders can gather information from the candle pattern suggesting towards sustained momentum in the direction of the existing trend when seen within a strong trend.

What is a Bullish Engulfing Candle?

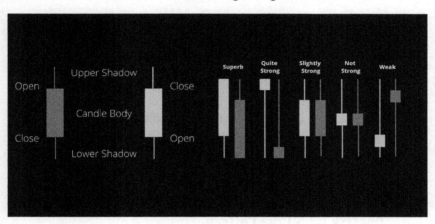

At the bottom of a downtrend, a bullish engulfing candle appears, signaling a spike in purchasing pressure. The bullish engulfing pattern frequently signals a trend reversal as additional buyers enter the market to push prices upward. The pattern consists of two candles, the second of which entirely engulfs the previous red candle's body.

What is a Bullish Engulfing Pattern, and How Do I See One?

- A large green candle that engulfs the previous red candle (disregard the wicks).
- Occurs when a downhill trend comes to an end.

- When the red candle is a Doji or following candles close above the high of the bullish candle, the signal is stronger.

What does this mean for traders?

- An upward trend reversal (bullish reversal)
- At this critical level, selling pressure is waning.

The benefits of trading with a bullish engulfing **candle are as follows:**

- Simple to recognize
- After gaining confirmation of the bullish reversal, attractive entry levels can be gained.

Know the Difference Between a Bullish and a Bearish Engulfing Pattern.

Bullish and bearish engulfing patterns exist.

The bearish engulfing pattern is the polar opposite of the bullish engulfing pattern mentioned previously. It appears near the top of an upswing rather than in a downtrend and gives traders a signal to go short. A green candle gets absorbed by a larger red candle in this pattern.

Trading with a Bullish Engulfing Candlestick Pattern

Forex Trading and Bullish Engulfing

The signal was confirmed by subsequent candles closing above the peak of the bullish candle. Stops can be placed below the low of the bullish engulfing pattern, with a target set at a critical level that price has already bounced off — this is the current swing high, and the risk-to-reward ratio is favorable.

Stock Trading and Bullish Engulfing

Bullish engulfs is a popular forex strategy that may also be used in the stock market. When trading the bullish engulfing candle, complementing the candle formation with a supporting signal/indicator is crucial to developing confidence. Before completing a deal, tock traders can rely on these supporting signs for more confidence.

The stop loss can be set below the most recent swing low, which is the Dragonfly Doji's low. The target (limit) can be set at a crucial level where the price has previously bounced, as long as the risk-to-reward ratio is good.

What is a Bearish Engulfing Pattern?

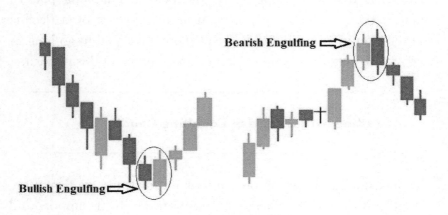

When a bearish engulfing pattern comes at the end of an upswing, it produces the strongest indication. The design is made by combining the data from two finished candles:

The first candle will depict the end of the established trend strength. The size of this primary/bullish candle can vary, but the body of this candle must be totally 'engulfed' by the next flame. The clearest signal to show market hesitation in the current trend is Dojis and other minor bullish candles.

The reversal signal is the second candle in the pattern. This candle is made up of a long red candle that is causing a new downward price trend. This bearish candle should open above the closing of the previous candle and close considerably below the low of the preceding candle. This sharp decline implies selling outnumbering buyers, and it frequently signals a price drop to come. The stronger the indication becomes when this secondary/ bearish candle falls further.

Know the Difference Between a Bearish and a Bullish Engulfing Pattern.

Bullish and bearish engulfing patterns exist. The bullish engulfing pattern is the polar opposite of the bearish engulfing pattern mentioned previously. It appears near the bottom of a decline rather than in an uptrend and gives traders a signal to go long. A red candle gets absorbed by a larger green flame in this pattern.

Trading with a Bearish Engulfing Candle

Traders should always be on the lookout for trade confirmation, whether it's through indicators, important levels of support and resistance, or any other method that might validate or invalidate a trade. Two techniques to strengthening the bearish bias provided by the bearish engulfing pattern are presented below.

Using Indicators to Trade the Bearish Engulfing Candle

While trading against the trend is not recommended, reversals do happen, which is why all traders should be able to recognize when this is likely to happen.

Traders can enter by waiting for a closing lower than the bearish candle's low or placing working orders far below the low.

> **Stop-loss:** Place a stop above the current swing high to invalidate the move and give a modest risk-to-reward ratio.

Because bearish engulfing candles can signal the start of a long-term decline, it's a good idea to set an initial take-profit level while keeping an eye on the future downward movement. Consider utilizing a trailing stop or adjusting your stops accordingly.

Using Support and Resistance to Trade the Bearish Engulfing Candle

The amount of support is significant since it indicates that higher moves have previously been rejected. When the bearish bearing engulfing pattern appears at resistance, it strengthens the bearish bias.

Traders may consider joining the trade at the open of the next candle if the bearish engulfing is supported by the level of resistance.

Stop: Place the stop above the bearish engulfing candle and the resistance level. A move higher than this would nullify the move.

Targets and take-profit levels can be placed at current support levels. The bearish engulfing candle may signify the start of a persistent slump; therefore, traders should consider a second target level – or use a trailing stop.

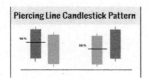

What Is A Piercing Pattern?

A t the bottom of a downtrend, the piercing line pattern appears as a bullish reversal candlestick pattern.

As bulls enter the market and push prices higher, it frequently results in a trend reversal.

The piercing pattern consists of two bullish candlesticks, the second of which opens lower than the preceding bearish candle.

This is followed by buyers forcing prices higher to close over 50% of the bearish candle's body.

How to Identify a Piercing Pattern on Forex Charts?

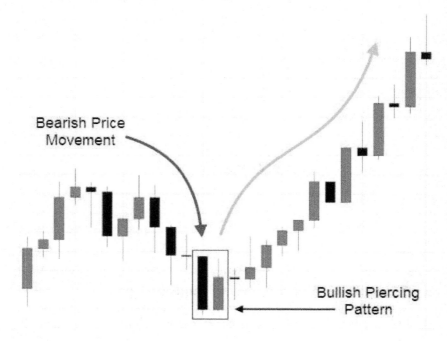

A piercing pattern's **characteristics include:**

- It happens at the bottom of a downward trend.
- Contains both a bearish and a bullish candle
- The bullish candle opens lower than the bearish candle's closure.
- The bullish candle then closes above the bearish candle body's 50% level.

So, what does this mean for traders?

- Possibility of an upward trend reversal (bullish reversal)
- At this important price level, the bears (sellers) are losing steam.

The benefits of trading with a **bullish engulfing candle are as follows:**

- Both newbie and experienced traders will find it easy to identify.
- Possibility of advantageous risk-to-reward ratios
- Once the piercing pattern has been confirmed, desirable entry levels can be reached.

Piercing Line Pattern for Trading

A significant downturn preceded this pattern, as seen by lower lows and lower highs. This example shows how price action may be used to identify a downturn. On the other hand, traders frequently choose to use a technical indicator for confirmation, such as the moving average (price needs to be above the long-term moving average).

As previously said, more confirmation of the piercing pattern is required before getting into a long trade. The RSI oscillator was employed as further confirmation of a reversal in this scenario. The RSI provides an oversold signal on the chart, confirming the integrity of the piercing pattern.

Stop levels can be set at the most recent low (bottom of the bullish piercing pattern candle), and take profit (limit) levels can be found using Fibonacci extensions or price movement.

What is the Reliability of the Piercing Line?

Piercing line patterns indicate bullish reversals; however, relying solely on this pattern is not advised. Other support signals in conjunction with the piercing pattern might be beneficial.

Trading against a dominating trend can be dangerous; thus, collecting several confirmation signals to corroborate the pattern is recommended.

What is a Dark Cloud Cover Pattern?

The Dark Cloud Cover pattern is a candlestick pattern that indicates a possible downside reversal. A massive green (bullish) candle appears at the top of an uptrend, followed by a red (bearish) candle that establishes a new high before closing lower than the midpoint of the previous green candle.

Although quite similar, this candle formation should not be mistaken with the Bearish Engulfing candle pattern. Both patterns indicate a possible trend reversal, but the Dark Cloud Cover has more appealing entry levels because the bearish candle closes higher than the bearish engulfing candle pattern.

How to Identify a Dark Cloud on Forex Charts?

Checklist for **Dark Cloud Cover:**

1. Determine whether or not there is an established uptrend.
2. Keep an eye out for signs that progress is slowing or reversing (stochastic oscillators, bearish moving average crossover, or subsequent bearish candle formations).
3. Stocks will gap up, with the red candle opening above the preceding green candle; however, this is quite rare in FX candlesticks, as these candles will usually open at the same level as, or very near to, the previous candle's close.
4. Make sure the red candle closes lower than the previous green candle's midpoint.
5. Keep an eye out for evidence of the new downward trend.

How to Use the Dark Cloud Pattern in Trading

Traders can use Dark Cloud Cover technical analysis in range markets to trade more classic trending markets like the GBP/USD or EUR/USD.

To evaluate a potential deal, apply this **Dark Cloud Cover checklist:**

1. The presence of higher highs and lower lows indicates an upward trend.
2. The market had begun to move more sideways on the chart since the most recent upward rise initially

meandered sideways, and when it did move up, it was not as dramatic as previously recorded. Furthermore, the RSI rose into the overbought area, indicating that the trade is more confident.

3. The red candle is slightly higher than the green candle before it. The candle will usually open at the same level as the previous close in the FX market.
4. The red bearish candle falls lower and closes below the bullish candle's midpoint, indicating that the bears are outnumbering the bulls at that time.
5. The very next candle and successive candles show confirmation of sustained selling (downward pressure). Lower highs and lower lows indicated that the market had successfully reversed, and a downtrend had been established.

When glancing at the chart, entry levels, goals, and stops are all plainly visible. After the Dark Cloud Cover pattern has been established, the entry can be made at the open of the next candle.

Stops can be placed above the latest swing high, and the initial target level can be set at critical levels or recent support/resistance zones. It's worth noting that traders might select numerous target levels because the transaction could be the start of a longer downtrend.

Ranging markets

When the price tends to 'bounce' between support and resistance in a ranging market, a similar method can be used. The Dark Cloud Cover pattern, which appears around resistance, is a short indication that could convert into a breakthrough trade if there is enough momentum.

The Dark Cloud's Benefits and Limitations

Like all other candlestick patterns, the validity of the Dark Cloud is determined by the market activity surrounding it, indicators, where it appears in the trend, and important levels of resistance.

What Are Harami Candlesticks, Exactly?

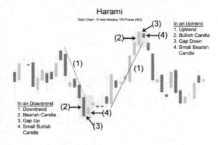

The Harami candlestick is a two-candle Japanese candlestick pattern that suggests a potential market reversal or continuation.

The word 'Harami' comes from the Japanese word 'pregnant,' which describes the Harami candlestick pattern. The Harami candlestick pattern can signal both bullish and bearish signals.

Bullish Harami

---

1. A downward trend has been established.
2. The larger bearish (red) candle in front of it.
3. Trailing smaller bullish (green) candle - price gaps up

following a bearish candle and are contained within the leading bearish candle's open and close.

Bearish Harami

---

1. An upward trend has been established.
2. The larger bullish (green) candle in front of it.
3. Trailing smaller bearish (red) candle - price widens down following a bullish candle and is contained within the leading bullish candle's open and close.

The first candle (pregnant candle) is a giant candle that continues the current trend, while the trailing candle is a small candle that protrudes from the market like a pregnant lady. It's worth noting that the second candle will technically gap inside the first. Gapping on forex charts, on the other hand, is uncommon due to the 24-hour nature of currency trading. As a result, the theoretically perfect Harami is uncommon in the FX market, as gaps are narrow, and the second candle frequently forms a small inside bar of the first.

The confirming candle is used to inform traders whether the smaller trailing candle initiates a reversal or continues to follow the trend established by the starting candle. The Harami pattern's and other candlestick patterns' popularity stems from its ability to catch a reversal at the most appropriate time with minimal risk. Traders will be able to achieve exceptionally favorable risk-reward ratios as a result of this.

Uses of the Harami Candle in Forex Trading

The Harami pattern has the **following advantages**

- Simple to recognize
- Possibility of profiting from significant fluctuations with high risk-to-reward ratios
- It's widely used in the currency market.

Harami's **drawbacks include the following**

- Prior to execution, confirmation is required.

Trading With Harami Candle Pattern

Depending on the validating candle, the Harami candlestick pattern can produce both bullish and bearish signs. Both forms of Harami patterns and how they appear in the currency market are depicted in the forex charts below.

Traders can use other technical indicators to support candlestick patterns in most cases. It's crucial to keep in mind that not all Harami patterns predict reversals.

Bearish Harami

Reversal signs are generally stronger (support, resistance, highs, and lows).

The context is critical when traders interpret Harami candles. Analyzing past charting patterns (trends) and price action will provide the trader with more information and capacity to predict the Harami pattern's ramifications. The Harami is only three practically tiny candles when taken out of context.

Patterns for Harami Candlestick and Reversal

- In technical trading, reversal patterns are particularly popular because they allow traders to profit from changes in market trends.

Why The Harami candlestick is easily identifiable and can detect a reversal pattern at the most reasonable risk.

- Harami reversals can assist traders in detecting clear bias and risk points in this way.

The Harami is one of the most popular reversal candle patterns. The Harami, like most candlestick formation patterns, offers a tale about market emotion in real-time. You can turn to the next candle to find a definite bias and risk points after the pattern is completed with the closing of the signal candle.

Why Do Traders Desire Reversal Patterns?

Reversal patterns and continuation patterns are the two types of candlestick trading indications. Traders can use continuation patterns to detect when sentiment is likely to keep the current trend going strong.

Reversal patterns can assist traders spot when a trend's sentiment is likely to wane when the pair reverses direction. The information from buyers and sellers that indicates these potential reversals is contained in the creation of the candles. Understanding and recognizing reversal candlestick patterns such as the Harami can help traders profit from trend shifts.

Using the Harami Candlestick to Catch Reversals

The Harami candlestick pattern is popular because it helps traders to catch a reversal at the right time with minimal risk. As a result, risk-to-reward ratios might be highly favorable. To use the Harami to spot reversal patterns, traders must first grasp the candlestick's origins and how it can be combined with other technical indicators.

Harami's Supporting Functions

Traders are rapidly introduced to the Doji candlestick when studying candlestick trading to determine market turning events. The most basic premise and the first lesson concern the appearance of the Doji candlestick, which might indicate a potential reversal and a good opportunity to enter a trade.

The following candle tells the story about the trade preference you should have, even though Doji is just made up of one candle that opens and closes near the same level and has an upper and lower wick out of the body like a "+" sign.

Once a Doji has formed, other oscillating indicators or moving averages can be used to determine if the pair is in an extreme state or not. This shows when candlestick formations are the most effective.

The Harami gets its name from the fact that it resembles a pregnant woman. The Doji is a small candle that protrudes like a pregnant woman, and the first candle is a large candle that continues the current trend. The second candle will reveal if the

Doji initiates a reversal or continues the trend established by the first candle.

Traders who want to profit from the Bearish Harami pattern can include it in any existing trend trading strategy. Once this pattern develops, traders can take profits on any existing long trades or even contemplate trading a full-fledged reversal. When adding new components to a strategy, traders should keep note of their performance in a trade journal, regardless of the trading plan. Traders can assess the success of price action and candle analysis in trading over time in this fashion.

What is a Bullish Harami Pattern?

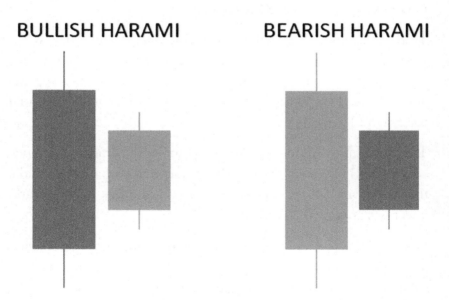

BULLISH HARAMI   BEARISH HARAMI

A reversal pattern that appears at the bottom of a downtrend is the Bullish Harami candle pattern. A bearish candle with a large body is followed by a bullish candle with a small body encompassed within the body of the previous candle. The little bullish candle' gaps' up to open towards the mid-range of the previous candle as a sign of changing momentum.

The Bearish Harami, which is observed near the top of an uptrend, is the polar opposite of the Bullish Harami.

Bullish Harami Cross

Traders will frequently seek for a Doji as the second candle in a pattern. The reason for this is that the Doji represents market hesitation. The color of the Doji candle (black, green, or red) is unimportant because the bullish indication is provided by the Doji itself, which appears near the bottom of a downtrend. Because the bullish trend (once confirmed) is just getting started, the Bullish Harami Cross offers an appealing risk to return potential.

How to Identify a Bullish Harami on Trading Charts

The Bullish Harami will appear differently on a stock chart than it will on a 24-hour forex chart, but the same techniques for identifying the pattern will apply.

Checklist for Bullish Harami:

1. Recognize an existing downward trend.
2. Keep an eye out for signs that progress is slowing or reversing (stochastic oscillators, bullish moving average crossover, or subsequent bullish candle formations).
3. Ensure the small green candle's body is no more than 25% of the previous bearish candle's body. Stocks will gap higher, with the green candle appearing in the

middle of the previous candle. The two candles will usually be displayed side by side on forex charts.

4. Notice how the full body of the previous bearish candle is enclosed within the length of the bullish candle.

5. Use supportive indicators or important levels of support to look for confluence.

In the Forex market, the Bullish Harami Pattern is forming.

When one candle closes, another opens at about the same level as the previous candle's closing price in the FX market, which runs 24 hours a day, five days a week. During normal market conditions, this is common, but it can change during moments of severe volatility.

The Bullish Harami Pattern Types on Stock Charts

On the other hand, Stocks have set trading hours throughout the day and are known to gap at the open for a variety of reasons. **Some of them could be:**

- News about the company is released after the market closes.
- Economic data by country/sector
- Rumored mergers or takeover bids
- The general mood of the market

How to Trade the Bullish Harami Candlestick Pattern?

Traders can use the five-step checklist outlined earlier in this section to implement the Bullish Harami.

1. There is a distinct downward tendency.

2. A Bullish Hammer appears before the Bullish Harami and provides the first clue that the market may be about to reverse.

3. The bullish candle is no longer than 25% of the previous candle's length.

4. The bullish candle is the same length as the previous candle when it opens and closes.

5. The market is oversold, according to the RSI. This could indicate that bearish momentum is slowing, but traders should wait for confirmation from the RSI crossing back over the 30 lines.

Stops can be placed below the new bottom, and traders can enter at the open of the candle after the Bullish Harami pattern has been completed. Traders might include numerous target levels to ride out a freshly extended uptrend because the Bullish Harami appears at the commencement of a possible uptrend. These targets can be set at current support and resistance levels.

Can the Bullish Harami Be Trusted?

Like that all other forex candlestick patterns, the Bullish Harami's validity is determined by the market action surrounding it, the indications that show in the trend, and important levels of support. The following are some of the pattern's benefits and drawbacks.

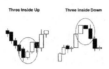

8

Three Inside Up   Three Inside Down

Three-Candle Pattern

Morning Star

T he Morning Star candlestick is a three-candle pattern that can be employed when trading forex or any other market to signal a market reversal. When trading financial markets, correctly recognizing reversals is critical because it allows traders to enter at attractive levels at the very beginning of a possible trend reversal.

What is a Morning Star Candlestick?

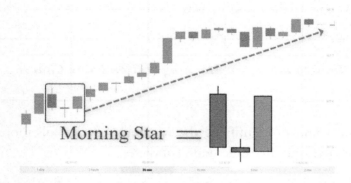

At the bottom of a downtrend, the Morning Star pattern is a three-candle bullish reversal candlestick pattern. It shows that downward momentum is diminishing before a major positive rise builds the groundwork for a new upswing.

Morning Star Doji Traders will often watch for signals of market hesitation, such as when selling pressure eases, and the market remains relatively level.

Doji candles can be seen when the market opens and closes at the same level or very near to the same level. This hesitation allows for a bullish rise, as bulls perceive value at this level and are unable to sell higher. The arrival of the bullish candle provides this bullish confirmation after the Doji.

What About the Evening Star?

The evening star is the bearish equivalent of the Morning Star, and it denotes a potential market turning point in a rising market (bearish reversal pattern). The same analysis that was applied to the Morning Star can be applied to the Evening Star. It will, however, be in the opposite way.

How to Identify a Morning Star on Forex Charts

On forex charts, identifying the Morning Star entails more than just recognizing the three main candles.

Understanding previous price action and where the pattern emerges within the current trend is necessary.

1. Determine if there is an existing downtrend: The market should have lower highs and lower lows.

2. Large bearish candle: A large bearish candle is formed when there is a lot of selling pressure and the downturn continues. There is no evidence of a reversal at this time; therefore, traders should only be searching for short bets.

3. Small bearish/bullish candle: The second candle is small - commonly referred to as a Doji candle - and represents the first hint of downward exhaustion. As it makes a lower low, this candle frequently gaps lower. The major message here is that the market is somewhat uncertain, regardless of whether the candle is bearish or bullish.

4. Large bullish candle: This candle shows the first real hint of new purchasing pressure. This candle gaps up from the preceding candle's closing in non-forex markets, signaling the start of a new uptrend.

5. Price activity after a successful reversal: Traders will notice higher highs and lower lows after a successful reversal.

Still, they should always control the danger of a failed move by using well-placed stops.

Instructions on How to Trade the Morning Star Pattern

Traders can look to enter at the open of the next candle if the formation is complete. More cautious traders may want to wait and see whether market movement moves higher before entering. However, this has the disadvantage of allowing the trader to enter at a much lower level, which is especially true in fast-moving markets.

Previous levels of resistance or areas of consolidation can be used as targets. Stops might be set below the previous swing low, as a break of this level invalidates the reversal.

Because the forex market offers no guarantees, traders should always practice solid risk management while keeping a favorable risk-to-reward ratio.

Because the price of the Morning Star on forex markets rarely gaps as it does in stocks, the three-candle pattern frequently opens extremely near to the previous closing level.

How Reliable is the Morning Star in Forex Trading?

When looking at an indicator, the Morning Star, like most candlestick patterns, should be evaluated in light of the current trend and whether there is supporting data in favor of the trade.

What is an Evening Star Candlestick?

At the apex of an uptrend, the Evening Star pattern is a three-candle bearish reversal candlestick pattern.

It indicates that upward momentum is waning before a bearish move builds the groundwork for a new decline.

How to Identify an Evening Star on Forex Charts

On forex charts, identifying the Evening Star entails more than just recognizing the three main candles. Understanding previous price action and where the pattern emerges within the current trend is necessary.

1. Determine whether or not there is an existing uptrend: The market should have higher highs and lower lows.

2. Enormous bullish candle: The large bullish candle is the outcome of strong purchasing pressure and the uptrend's continuation. There is no evidence of a reversal at this point, so traders should just be searching for long trades.

3. Small bearish/bullish candle: The second candle is small, frequently referred to as a Doji candle, and it is the first indicator of a weary upswing. As it makes a greater high, this candle frequently gaps higher. The major message here is that the market is somewhat uncertain, regardless of whether the candle is bearish or bullish.

4. Large bearish candle: This candle shows the first real hint of new selling pressure. This candle gaps down from the previous candle's closure in non-forex markets, signaling the start of a new downturn.

5. Price action after a successful reversal: Traders will notice lower highs and lower lows after a successful reversal, but they should always control the danger of a failed move by using well-placed stops.

Traders will often watch for signals of market hesitancy, such as a drop in purchasing pressure that leaves the market flat. This is the perfect spot for a Doji candle to show up.

Evening Star Doji

Doji candles are formed when the market opens and closes at the same level or extremely close to it. This hesitation allows for a bearish move, as bears sense value at this level and are unable to buy more. The arrival of the bearish candle provides this bearish confirmation after the Doji.

What Do You Think About the Morning Star?

The Morning Star is a bullish variation of the Evening Star that indicates a potential turning point in a falling market (bullish reversal pattern). The Morning Star can be subjected to the same analysis as the Evening Star. It will, however, be in the opposite way.

How to Trade the Evening Star Candlestick Pattern

Keep an eye out for the evening star formation. Traders might look to enter at the open of the next candle once the formation is complete. More cautious traders may want to wait and see whether market action moves lower before entering. However, this has the disadvantage of allowing the trader to enter at a much lower level, which is especially true in fast-moving markets.

Previous levels of support or areas of consolidation can be used as targets. Stops should be put above the previous swing high, as a break of this level would nullify the reversal. Because the forex market offers no guarantees, traders should always practice solid risk management while keeping a favorable risk-to-reward ratio.

Because the price of the Evening Star on forex markets rarely gaps as it does in stocks, the three-candle pattern frequently opens extremely near to the previous closing level.

How Reliable is the Evening Star in Forex Trading?

When looking at an indicator, the Evening Star, like most candlestick patterns, should be evaluated in light of the current trend and whether there is supporting data in favor of the trade.

9

Candlestick Vs. Heikin Ashi

What are Heikin-Ashi Candlesticks?

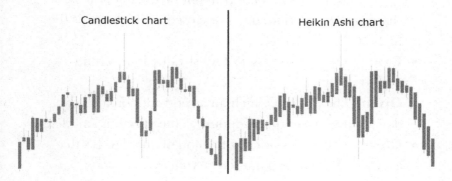

Candlestick chart   Heikin Ashi chart

Heikin-Ashi literally translates to "Average Bar" in Japanese, which is exactly what these candlesticks are. The Heikin-Ashi candlesticks derive the necessary charts by combining average highs, lows, open, and closes and removing numerous extreme units in the process. This filtering reduces market noise and significant variations, making them much easier to understand.

This tool, along with regular candlesticks, can help you recognize market trends, anticipate future values for various securities, and make more confident investing decisions.

The Heikin-Ashi candlesticks are a modified version of ordinary candles that are often employed in the commodities market. They have some similarities to traditional candles, but they use a modified formula of close-open-high-low that the price makes during the course of the period. The candlesticks show not only the movement of the selected period but also historical price data.

The four sections of the Heikin-Ashi candlestick are listed below, along with their formula:

- **High:** This refers to the actual high of the time period - the highest price reached. It might be the highest shadow in the period, open or closed – whichever is the highest.
- **Low:** It denotes the asset's lowest value in a certain period of time.
- **Open:** The price at which an asset trades on a given day (equivalent to the midpoint of the previous candle.)
- **Close:** The asset's price at the end of the day. It's the average of the four parameters' values.

What's the Difference Between Heikin-Ashi and Regular Candlesticks?

Although they appear to be similar at first glance, Heikin Ashi and normal candlesticks have a number of differences. Heikin-Ashi candlesticks can be constructed in the same way as conventional candlesticks. The formula for each bar, however, is different. Because regular candlesticks are based on actual values, their trends are more volatile and erratic.

Average Heikin Ashi measurements, on the other hand, prune out extreme values, resulting in smoother candlesticks and more steady trends. During a downtrend and an uptrend, the Heiken-Ashi candlesticks also tend to alternate between red and green. On the other hand, regular candlesticks take turns with the colors even if the price moves strongly in one way. - As a result, Heikin-Ashi is said to be easier to read than the former.

Heikin Ashi candlesticks use two-period averages to generate trends in a time series, whereas normal candlesticks use actual prices to drive trends.

However, this has the drawback of occasionally obliterating key information concerning price action. In addition, Heikin Ashi trends have inconsistent gaps in their patterns, whereas normal candlesticks have more stable gaps. Traditional candles have a history of displaying multiple uptrends or downtrends in a row.

Heikin Ashi candles are noted for having identical trends in a row, making pricing patterns easier to spot.

Instructions for Using Heikin-Ashi

Because Heikin-Ashi charts can be used in a variety of markets, most platforms feature this tool as an option. Heikin-Ashi charts, on the whole, have reasonably consistent trends — their uptrends and downtrends do not change as much as normal candles. The Heikin-Ashi candles, as seen in the charts above, depict continuous uptrends/downtrends, but conventional candles do not.

Heikin-Ashi typically provides five major indications to help you pick out the best buy and sell chances from a sea of trends.

A consistently sinking market is indicated by red or filled candles without shadows; it is best to stay short and wait for the down-trend to change before entering. Similarly, filled or red candles indicate a downtrend and indicate that short trades should be entered and long positions should be exited. Green or hollow candles with no top wick or shadows, on the other hand, indicate a strong uptrend, so ride it and maximize your earnings. Add long positions and short exit positions when you detect simple green or hollow candles.

A change in trend is indicated by candles with smaller bodies and relatively lengthy upper and lower wicks. This period of transition may be deemed unsafe; novices should stay away at this time and wait for a solid trend to emerge before returning to the game. Investors with a higher risk appetite, on the other hand, can take advantage of the trend to purchase or sell.

Heikin-Ashi candlesticks are simple to use and understand. For traders and investors, they provide a comprehensive picture of the market. They are adequate for comprehending current market conditions and assisting in trend predictions. Heikin Ashi candlesticks can be used in conjunction with normal candlesticks because of their ease of representation of trends. They filter out extreme measurements while reducing market noise to create smoother, more legible trends.

However, this has the drawback of causing the loss of some crucial data as well as large irregular gaps in the trends.

Nonetheless, the benefits of these candles greatly exceed the disadvantages, which is why they are still one of the most often utilized trading tools today.

How to Use Heikin-Ashi Patterns to Evaluate and Identify Trends

Heikin-Ashi Candlesticks are a powerful tool that chartists can use to filter noise, predict reversals, and identify classic chart patterns. All parts of traditional technical analysis and charting are supported. Heikin-Ashi Candlesticks are used by chartists to define support and resistance, establish trend lines, and quantify retracements. Indicators of volume and momentum oscillators are also useful. Heikin Ashi charts are frequently employed as a technical indicator to help emphasize and clarify the current trend on a traditional candlestick chart.

Swing traders and investors use Heikin Ashi charts on occasion. Heikin Ashi charts are more commonly used as an indication by day traders, as they have a number of advantages.

Trends and buying opportunities are **identified by five basic signals:**

- Uptrends are indicated by green candles.
- A strong rise is indicated by green candles with no lower "shadows."
- A trend change is indicated by candles with a small body surrounded by upper and lower shadows.
- A downturn is indicated by red candles.
- A significant downturn is indicated by red candles with no upper shadows.

A Heiken Ashi trader is looking for two signals:

- A green candle with no bottom shadow, indicating a strong bullish indicator.
- A red candle with no top shadow, which indicates a strong bearish indicator.

When compared to typical candlesticks, these signals may make identifying trends or trading opportunities easier. Trends are less frequently disrupted by misleading signals, making them easier to recognize.

Heiken Ashi Candle Patterns and Types

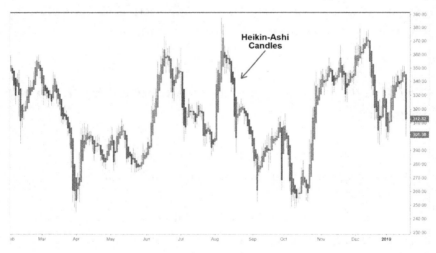

The size of the candle's body, shadows, and range define whether the candle is bullish, bearish, or neutral.

1. continuation candles - little candles with a narrow range

2. Candles with a strong uptrend - candles with a wide range but no tail
3. candles with a strong downtrend
4. The indecisive candle has a small body, a long tail, and a shadow on both sides. These indicate a shift in the trend or a pause in the trend.
5. Candle with a Doji
6. A top candle that spins
7. Candles with no shadow are known as bearish candles.

The common patterns formed on the Heikin Ashi chart include Doji Reversal Candlestick Triangle Pattern Patterns of Rising and Falling Wedge.

The initiation candle establishes the tone of the trend and determines the price's underlying momentum. In Trend Analysis and Price Action Trading, this is why Initiation Candles are so crucial. Continuation candles reaffirm the trend's direction and can be used to boost positions in that direction.

Heikin-Ashi Doji and Spinning Tops

Heikin-Ashi Doji and spinning tops, like regular candlesticks, can be used to predict reversals. A Heikin-Ashi Doji or Heikin-Ashi spinning top resembles a regular Doji or spinning top in appearance.

- A Doji is a little candlestick with nearly identical open and closing values. Little price movement is indicated by little upper and lower shadows.
- Spinning tops have small bodies with long upper/lower

135

shadows (open-close range) (high-low range). Despite multiple swings from high to low, prices end up close to where they started for little change. This demonstrates indecision, which could indicate a turnaround.

A Doji or spinning top in a downtrend should not be interpreted as bullish when utilizing Heikin-Ashi candlesticks. It simply demonstrates indecisiveness within the downturn. The first step toward a new course is indecision.

However, confirmation of a directional change (trend reversal) is necessary. It's important to designate a resistance level for a trend reversal whenever chartists notice a Doji or spinning top in a downtrend.

Heiken-Ashi Trading Strategies

When trading with Heiken Ashi Candles, **there are essentially five patterns to follow.**

1. A strong rise is indicated by green candles with no lower shadows: Be in the trade when you see these on the charts and don't think about profit booking. You could wish to increase the length of your lengthy position and the length of your short exit position.

2. Trend change is indicated by candles with a tiny body and upper and lower shadows: These are indecisive candles that need to be confirmed.

3. A significant downturn is indicated by green/red candles with no upper shadow: Be in the trade when you see these on the charts and don't think about profit booking. You might wish to increase the length of your short and long exit positions.

4. Buying interest is represented by candles with lengthy lower shadows. Always keep an eye out for these candles and evaluate price movement after spotting them.

5. Candles with lengthy upper shadows indicate selling interest; if you see such Candles, be wary of existing long holdings.

Price action rules should be included in every **Heikin Ashi trading system:**

- Look for levels of support and resistance.
- Keep an eye out for chart patterns that could indicate a breakout.
- Get in on burgeoning trends and get out on fading ones.

It is easier to validate the trend when Heiken Ashi is used in conjunction with momentum indicators. A Heiken Ashi moving average method would watch for candles to cross over a 50-period moving average as an entry signal.

If you were waiting to buy after an upward crossover, the following confirming candle would be a bullish candle; if you were waiting to sell after an upward crossover, the next confirming candle would be a bearish candle.

You might also utilize an Ichimoku cloud. Ichimoku cloud, also known as Ichimoku Kinko Hyo, is a trend-following strategy based on candlesticks. Although it was created with standard candlesticks in mind, some traders choose to utilize Heiken Ashi candles instead. This Ichimoku Heiken Ashi combo can help you improve your strategy and stay on track.

Heikin-Ashi Techniques

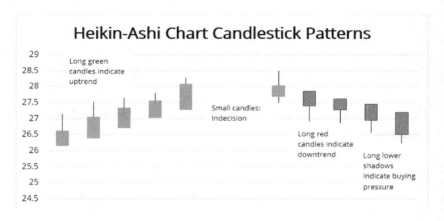

The following are some Heikin-Ashi tactics that traders can use to boost their profits and margins.

- ***Establishment of a Strong Bullish or Bearish Trend.***

Identifying the start of a strong upswing or downward trend is the most typical tactic for the Heikin-Ashi technique. Heikin-Ashi signal indicators are generally thought to be quite trustworthy and are only seldom erroneous.

As a result of the Heikin-Ashi trend signal's reliability, traders can profitably ride the trend. Traders with short holdings should withdraw if a bullish trend emerges, while those with long positions should raise and consolidate their positions.

- ***Determine whether or not there are any candlesticks with no shadows.***

Finding candlesticks with no shadows is a reliable indicator that a powerful bullish trend is about to begin. Because of its track record and high success rate, this method is one of the most popular Heikin-Ashi strategies.

The stronger the predicted trend, the longer the series of candlesticks with no tails. Similarly, traders could expect a new stable downward bearish trend to continue if candlesticks with no upper shadows are identified.

- *Small-bodied candlesticks indicate trend pauses or reversals.*

Traders should be aware of and pay attention to the advent of candles with small bodies. When a trend is going to pause or reverse, these candles are utilized to signal it. As a result, when traders realize this, they react by opening new positions in response to the trend ending.

Traders should use caution since the trend may be pausing rather than reversing. In that circumstance, the trader's skill is essential to assess whether a trend reversal is imminent or simply a trend pause.

The Heikin-Ashi Technique's Advantages

1. Accessibility: Heikin-Ashi is one of the most accessible indicators because it does not require any installation and can be found on any trading platform.

2. High chart readability: Any trader can understand the candlestick patterns, making them simple to interpret. Heikin-Ashi candlesticks are easier to read than typical candlestick charts, making market trends and movements easier to spot.

3. Reliability: Heikin-Ashi is a highly dependable indicator that consistently produces correct findings. It is based on historical data, which is also quite reliable.

4. Market noise filtering: The indicator eliminates tiny corrections and filters out market noise, making the signals more visible. The smoothing effect makes identifying trends easier. Because today's markets are noisy, the Heikin-Ashi approach helps traders plan their entry and exit locations more efficiently by reducing noise.

5. Ability to combine with other indicators: The Heikin-Ashi indicator can be used in conjunction with other technical indicators to provide even more powerful market signals.

6. Timeframe agnostic: The technique can be applied to any time frame, including hourly, daily, monthly, and yearly. Larger time horizons, on the other hand, are more dependable.

Railway Tracks Pattern

The Railroad Track candlestick pattern is one of the best and most consistent candlestick patterns. The best thing about this pattern is that it can be used with any type of technical analysis. When paired with indicators or price action strategies, this pattern performs exceedingly well. It does not, however, generate buy/sell indications on its own.

I'll go through all of the strategies and tactics for trading railroad tracks utilizing price action analysis in this section.

Types of Railway Track Patterns

There are a variety of railway track patterns to choose from. Bullish railway track and Bearish railway track are the two types of railway track designs.

The Pattern of a Bearish Railway Track

The first candle in this pattern is bullish, whereas the second candle is bearish. If we try to read the pattern, we can see that the market started out bullish but ended up falling.

Interpretation

The market initially rises from a given price, signaling that buyers are interested in the currency. However, for whatever reason, the market drops back down to that price. This indicates that the purchasers are unwilling to pay a greater price for it. The final aspect of the interpretation will be discussed in the following sections.

The Pattern of a Bullish Railway Tracks

The bearish railway track pattern is the polar opposite of this pattern. The first candle is bearish, but the second candle is bullish in this case.

Interpretation

The first is bearish in this pattern, indicating that the sellers have some clout. On the other hand, the next candle becomes bullish, indicating that the buyers are refusing to allow the sellers to go down. If we look at it from the seller's point of view, the market's rapid recovery shows that sellers are not interested in selling at lower prices.

When should you be looking for the railway track pattern?

When it comes to trading candlestick patterns, this is one of the most often asked questions. Every timeline, after all, has its own story. As a result, it makes little difference on which timeframe you trade the pattern. And, if you're trading with price movement, the pattern will work across all timeframes.

What else is important?

When this pattern appears in a suitable location, it will work. Not all train tracks will follow your expected path. When the pattern functions according to its meaning, there are specific settings.

10

Trading Binary Options With Candlesticks

Every binary options trader should be aware of the following candlestick formations. The price data itself is the closest thing to the actual price, and the candlestick chart depicts current price data as well as its direct supply and demand dynamics, which translates into investors' attitudes. The candlestick formations seen below are particularly useful in binary options trading since they indicate an impending correction or trend change.

The Doji

A Doji can be any length, but the ideal one would have the identical opening and closing price, making it appear as thin as a thin line. It is insignificant if a Doji appears in a sideways market.

Even if it emerges alone and at the pinnacle of a trend, a cautious binary options trader should pay attention and prepare for a quick reversal. The presence of a Doji may signify a rapid correction or a trend change if you're utilizing Bollinger Bands and the price action is touching or beyond the bands. In both bullish and negative markets, the Doji can occur.

The Dragonfly Doji

When a Dragonfly Doji candle appears at the end of a down-trend, it is extremely bullish. It demonstrates that the sellers were able to lower the price but were unable to maintain the downward price movement because the price finished at the same level as it had opened.

This could signal an impending bullish trend and possibly a big upward trend. When a Dragonfly Doji crosses support resistance lines or Fibonacci retracement lines, the signal might be significantly stronger.

The Gravestone Doji

If the top shadow is quite long, it indicates a bearish feeling. Prices open and trade high for the candle's set time, then return to the opening price.

This pattern indicates that investors rallied but were unable to reach a higher price. This indicates a bearish attitude, and if this candle formation crosses resistance lines, Bollinger bands, or Fibonacci levels, it could indicate an impending reversal.

The Hammer

The genuine body of this design is modest, but the bottom shadow must be at least twice the length of the body. Hammers arise in downtrend markets, and their name comes from the fact that they are used to "hammer out the bottom" of the trend.

A Hammer indicates that, despite the pessimistic feeling, buyers may be able to push prices higher than the opening price. The failure of the sellers dampens bearish sentiment and could indicate a trend reversal.

The Hanging Man

The Hanging Man is similar to The Hammer, except it emerges at the peak of a trend or when the market is rising.

The price movement must trade substantially lower than the beginning price before rallying to close near the high in order for the Hanging Man to form. This creates a long lower shadow, which could indicate that the market is about to undergo a selloff and a possible reversal.

The real body of a Hanging Man with a black or red real body (depending on your candlestick setups) is more bearish than a complete or green body.

The Belt Hold – Bullish and Bearish

Two actual bodies of opposing colors make up a Belt Hold. It occurs when a market is trending, and a substantial gap opens in the trend's direction, but the trend then reverses. Bullish Belt Hold or Bearish Belt Hold candles move in the opposite direction, occasionally engulfing the previous candle and shifting the trend.

The Belt Hold candle formation denotes a shift in investor sentiment as well as a possible trend reversal and change.

The Harami Patterns

The Harami pattern, which is similar to the Belt Hold, can be bullish or bearish. It likewise has two candles with real bodies of the opposite hue, but the second candle's open price is inside the last candle's closure price. The second candle does not engulf the last candle as it does in The Belt Hold, despite the fact that it closes in the opposite direction. A stronger trend is indicated by the absence of an upper shadow (in a downward trend) or a lower shadow (in an upward trend) on the second candle.

How to Read Stock Charts Candlestick

One of the most popular strategies for stock traders to predict future market movements is to read stock market candlestick patterns. Despite the fact that the chart appears to be rather sophisticated at first glance, it can provide useful information about past stock market developments as well as information about trader conduct.

Stock trading candlestick patterns, in general, display information about the opening and closing positions, as well as high and low prices, for a given time period. The candlestick chart is most commonly used for day trading.

For technical analysis, candlestick charts are employed. Candlesticks are usually labeled with different colors, most often green and red or black and white. The colors represent various closing and opening points, as well as traders' sentiments, whether bullish or bearish. Traders can also learn about a specific asset's peak and lowest price by analyzing stock charts candlesticks.

Candlesticks on a stock chart are one of the most powerful instruments in the stock market. I

nvestors that base their strategy on technical analysis are the most likely to use it.

Start Trading In 10 Minutes

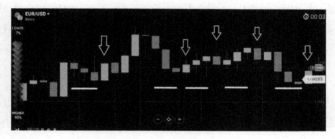

Apply everything you've learned on a real trading account with up to 1:777 leverage, negative balance protection, and exceptional customer service.

How to Read Candlestick Charts in Stocks

In stock trading, understanding chart candlesticks allows investors to gain more information about the market, allowing them to make more accurate predictions. Candlestick charts resemble bar charts in appearance but provide additional information.

To begin with, stock candlestick charts are made up of a lot of rectangles. Each rectangle is colored in two different hues alternately. The most common colors are green and red. The body is the fundamental component of the candlestick. On the candlestick, you can notice a line that looks like a median and divides the body into two equal pieces.

The upper part of this line is known as the upper shadow, while the bottom part is known as the lower shadow. It's important to know that investors can identify the first opening and last closing for a certain period, as well as high and low prices for a specific time through the body, while reading stock chart candlesticks. For example, if the candlestick chart is set to 5-minute intervals, each candlestick will display data for each 5-minute interval. Imagine two candlesticks, one green and the other red, to make it easier to understand.

Shadows, often known as tails or wicks, can be seen on the green body. The body is often green if the trader can observe the profit in a specific time span. If the wick, which comes from the rectangle's upper side and is longer than the line that comes from the rectangle's lower side, is longer than the wick, which comes from the rectangle's lower side, the net price is positive, and a trader in this period could make some winnings. If the body is dyed red, however, the situation is reversed, and the net price is negative.

Let's go over each component of a candlestick stock chart one by one to make reading it easier.

Opening and Closing Price

The candles, as previously said, reflect the purchasing and selling of a stock over a period of time. However, how can we tell which part of the candle is open and which is closed? Returning to the green and red candlesticks, let's say the green body indicates purchasing. That means it would start at the bottom of the body and open up from there. As a result, when the candle opens up right there, buyers would have pushed it up above, resulting in the green candle. The candlestick's open and close positions will be influenced by the direction in which the price is moving. If the price rises and closes higher than it started, the candlestick's opening position will be at the button. When the price falls, the exact reverse occurs. The top of the candlestick will be the open position, and the bottom will be the closing position.

Price: High & Low

The change in high prices may be seen in the wick, which is rising higher and higher above the candlestick body. The maximum price in a certain period is estimated by the last point of the shadow.

Assume the body opened up and was pushed up at some point, but the sellers forced it back down till it closed. As a result, your bottom wick will be short. As a result, it most likely opened up near the bottom of the body, and sellers tried to push it down, causing it to turn red.

Here's what happened in the event of the red candle and according to stock chart candlestick patterns. It most likely pushed up and turned green for a split second before sellers returned and said, "No, we're pushing this down." As a result, they drove it down, and it pushed below the open price of the red candle, and it sank, and it would have turned red as soon as it did.It came to a halt at a particular point. There were no purchasers that came in to push it up.

So it ended up closing at that moment at the end of that five-minute period, where the close price was lower.

Price Range & Direction

Traders can determine the price direction and range of an asset using information obtained from the candlestick chart. The wicks or shadows on the chart are used to measure price direction vertically. The open price is below the close price if the top line is longer than the one that emerges from the body's bottom side.

Investors can also use shadows and technical analysis to determine the best timing to buy or sell a given item. It's simple for them to assess if it's worth buying or selling an asset based on that information. Furthermore, due of the turbulent and liquid market, the price range differs between stocks and shares and can alter at any time.

Types of Candlesticks for Stock Trading

Candlestick patterns come in a variety of shapes and sizes. They are, however, classified into two groups: bullish and bearish. There are also subcategories within those primary categories. Bullish trends can arise after a market decline, signifying a price pattern rebound. They are a signal for investors to consider taking a long position in order to profit from an upward trend. A hammer, inverse hammer, bullish engulfing, piercing line, and the morning star are examples of bullish patterns.

Bearish candlestick patterns, on the other hand, occur after quick price gains in the stock market and subsequent skepticism about the market price, leading traders to liquidate long positions and start short ones in order to profit from the falling price. Hanging man, shooting star, and bearish engulfing are all bearish candlestick patterns.

Aside from that, there's a chart pattern that shows no market movement. Those types of charts are known as continuation candlestick patterns, and Doji is one of the most well-known and widely used of them.

Shooting Star

As previously stated, the shooting star is a bearish candlestick pattern. This pattern depicts an asset's upward trajectory. To return to the green and red candlesticks, suppose there are three green candles in the chart, which show investors' willingness to pay more and more for the stock. Once they realize they are overpaying for the asset, the color of the candle body changes to red, indicating that the closing price is no longer higher than the opening price. However, because it indicates the greatest price point in the chart, the red one followed by the three green bodies is dubbed a shooting star in this pattern.

Hammer

The hammer, unlike the shooting star, is a bullish candlestick pattern. It's ideal for traders who wish to start a long position. It displays when a particular asset begins to decline and the lowest price at which the stock might be purchased. The hammer is usually followed by the three red bodies, which display a wide variety of prices. Finally, traders conclude that the price will not go below a certain level, so they begin purchasing it to open a long position and selling it at a higher price to profit.

Bullish Engulfing

Two candlesticks, green and red, are required for the construction of a bullish engulfing pattern. The key premise behind this pattern is that when the second day starts lower than the first, the bullish market forces the price higher, giving the appearance of consumer success. The pattern is bullish, with one candlestick enveloping the other, and one candlestick's length being greater than the other's. Bullish engulfing happens at the bottom of a downtrend.

Bearish Engulfment

In contrast to the bullish engulfing, the bearish engulfing happens when the price of an asset begins to plummet following a rising trend. The trending candles, which are usually green in hue, usually follow the bearish engulfing candlestick. The red-colored pattern appears in the chart once the price begins to decline, engulfing the previous green-colored candlestick. Investors can use this pattern to track market fluctuations and determine an approximate peak in a stock's price as well as the point at which it plunged.

Doji

As previously stated, the Doji pattern denotes a situation in which the market values for a particular stock are nearly identical. Traders can see the plus or cross shape of the candlesticks in the Doji pattern by looking at the body and shadow.

A Doji pattern, which is regarded a neutral indication when there is no significant difference between the purchasing and selling prices, is easy to discern depending on that form. As a result, the net gain is nearly zero.

Conclusion

Trading stocks with candlestick charts have shown to be one of the most effective and successful methods of trading...when done correctly! It is simple to find basic information about candlestick charting techniques on the internet. Finding the whole narrative is a little more difficult.

There's no denying that candlestick trading is a popular topic among active stock traders. It's possible that it's one of the most explored topics on the internet when it comes to stock trading. The reasons are numerous, but the most important argument is that the technique works and many traders swear by their clear indications.

It can be extremely difficult for people who are new to candlesticks and are in the process of gathering information to put them together in an understandable fashion for traders to trade with. The majority of information on this type of trading is, at best, incomplete.

The patterns are simple to spot; however, figuring out how to trade them is a different story.

Candlestick pattern trading is a terrific option for any forex trader seeking a method that is both effective and simple to grasp and follow. Traders may design their own effective forex trading strategy by just learning and mastering a few key candlestick settings, allowing them to trade with clarity and conviction.

Many traders neglect the forex candlestick charts' simple power and overcomplicate their trading by adding other indicators to their charts, which simply complicates their trading and confuses their thoughts.

Do not fall prey to the misconception of lagging indicators like the bulk of wannabe forex traders; instead, build your trading confidence by learning to trade the forex market using forex candlestick patterns.

There are no patterns in bar charts that can be utilized to predict trend reversal or continuation. Whatever the case may be, it should be evident by now that candlestick charts are a far superior trading tool that you must grasp in order to understand price action.

Technical analysis and charting candlestick patterns are used by some traders. You can combine the RSI alongside candlestick patterns, for example, to confirm trade indications. To confirm your trading signals, combine a stochastic indicator with candlestick patterns.

You'll always be at the mercy of trading signals you don't comprehend if you don't learn these vital tools. Trading with those signals will only result in a series of losing trades. However, if you've mastered candlestick charting and technical analysis, you'll be able to confirm these trading indications and make more lucrative transactions.

Made in the USA
Las Vegas, NV
01 February 2022

42790737R00095